Counseling
and the
Human
Predicament

Psychology and Christianity
Edited by David G. Benner

Counseling
and the
Human
Predicament
A Study of Sin, Guilt, and Forgiveness

Edited by

LEROY ADEN
and
DAVID G. BENNER

BAKER BOOK HOUSE
Grand Rapids, Michigan 49516

Copyright 1989 by
Baker Book House Company

Printed in the United States of America

Library of Congress Cataloging-in-Publication Data

Counseling and the human predicament : a study of sin, guilt, and
    forgiveness / edited by LeRoy Aden and David G. Benner.
        p.   cm. — (Psychology and Christianity)
    Includes bibliographical references.
    ISBN 0-8010-0218-4
    1. Pastoral counseling.   2. Christianity—Psychology.   3. Man
(Christian theology)   4. Sin.   5. Guilt.   6. Forgiveness of sin.
I. Aden, LeRoy.   II. Benner, David G.   III. Series.
BV4012.2.C66   1989
253.5'2—dc20   89–38661
                                                                    CIP

Contents

Part 2 Guilt

Part 3 Forgiveness

Foreword to the Series

This volume is the third in the Psychology and Christianity Series, a collection of books published cooperatively by Baker Book House and the Christian Association for Psychological Studies (CAPS). Founded in 1952 in Grand Rapids, Michigan, by a group of psychologists, psychiatrists, and pastoral counselors, CAPS is an international society of Christian helping professionals committed to the exploration of the relationship between psychology and Christian faith.

Books in this series draw on previous CAPS publications and supplement these with original articles written for each volume. The purpose of the series is to present psychological and theological reflection on the most important issues encountered in human relationships, particularly relationships of counseling, education, parenting, and ministry.

Further information about the Christian Association for Psychological Studies may be obtained by contacting the head office:

Christian Association for Psychological Studies
P.O. Box 628
Blue Jay, CA 92317
(714) 337-5117

DAVID G. BENNER
Series Editor

7

Contributors

LeRoy Aden is Luther D. Reed Professor of Pastoral Care at the Lutheran Theological Seminary, Philadelphia, Pennsylvania.

Brad A. Binau is associate pastor at LaJolla Lutheran Church, LaJolla, California.

J. Harold Ellens is former executive secretary of the Christian Association for Psychological Studies and a pastoral theologian and psychotherapist in private practice.

Ralph Heynen at the time of retirement was hospital chaplain at Pine Rest Hospital, Grand Rapids, Michigan.

The late *Seward Hiltner* was emeritus professor of theology and personality at Princeton Theological Seminary, Princeton, New Jersey.

Lyman T. Lundeen is Ministerium of New York Professor of Systematic Theology at the Lutheran Theological Seminary, Philadelphia, Pennsylvania.

The late *O. Hobart Mowrer* was research professor of psychology at the University of Illinois, Urbana, Illinois.

S. Bruce Narramore is professor of psychology at the Rosemead Graduate School of Professional Psychology at La Mirada, California.

The late *E. Mansell Pattison* was professor of psychiatry and chairman of the department of the Medical College of Georgia, Augusta, Georgia.

Rinda G. Rogers is chaplain of the Artman Lutheran Home, Ambler, Pennsylvania.

Wendell Rooks is a retired psychiatrist who was in private practice in Grand Rapids, Michigan.

Introduction

LeRoy Aden

Nearly a century ago Sigmund Freud began to study the nature of the human predicament from a psychological perspective. His investigations led to a conscious and, in some circles of pastoral care, a concerted effort to relate psychological findings with theological affirmations. The attempt was new in the history of professional caring, for while there had always been some fruitful interchange between the church's and society's understandings of human nature, such communication had never been sustained and systematic. Now there was an intentional endeavor to investigate how insights derived from therapeutic psychology can illuminate theological concepts, and vice versa. The endeavor tended to move from psychology to theology more than in the other direction, since pastoral theorists, enamored of psychological findings, were eager to see theological concepts in a new and, perhaps, more invigorating light.

The relationship, in its many different forms, is now five or six decades old. It is time to take a critical look at the endeavor. Psychologists themselves have encouraged the inquiry. In 1973, Karl Menninger, a psychiatrist, asked the startling question, "Whatever became of sin?"[1] The question came out of his ob-

1. Karl Menninger, *Whatever Became of Sin?* (New York: Hawthorn, 1973).

servation that the psychological sciences and other humanistic developments had tended to override the theological concept, making it seem irrelevant, if not meaningless. Evil deeds were seen as crimes or sicknesses, falling into the domain of the lawyer or the psychiatrist, but they were no longer described as sins that required the ministrations of pastor or priest.

More than a decade earlier, O. Hobart Mowrer had registered a similar concern. He charged those engaged in Protestant pastoral care with exchanging their theological birthright for a bowl of psychological pottage.[2] Fifteen years after Mowrer's critique, Paul W. Pruyser was calling pastors back to their heritage by reassuring them that they possessed "a body of theoretical and practical knowledge that is uniquely their own, evolved over years of practice by themselves and their forebears."[3]

All three men sounded a needed alarm. They agreed that, at least in the decades of the 1960s and 1970s, psychology impinged on theological beliefs in a way that endangered the latter's distinctive domain. There were, of course, respected theorists who maintained that theology was being enlivened and enriched by psychological insights. Paul Tillich saw psychoanalytic psychology making a tremendous contribution to our understanding of human existence, especially in its "existential analysis of the human predicament."[4] David E. Roberts investigated the intersection of psychotherapy and Christian anthropology even more specifically and concluded that the Christian faith "can hardly be related effectively to the thought of this generation if it ignores or fails to comprehend the recent contributions which have been made to a 'science of man,'" especially since "some of the basic concepts of psychotherapy are correlative with the human side of events which Christian doctrine interprets."[5]

Authors can be quoted on either side of the issue. While we are not concerned about that fact here, it prompts us to reflect on the

2. See O. Hobart Mowrer, *The Crisis in Psychiatry and Religion* (Princeton: Van Nostrand, 1961), 60.

3. Paul W. Pruyser, *The Minister as Diagnostician* (Philadelphia: Westminster, 1976), 10.

4. Paul Tillich, "Existentialism, Psychotherapy, and the Nature of Man," in *The Nature of Man*, ed. Simon Doniger (New York: Harper, 1962), 46.

5. David E. Roberts, *Psychotherapy and a Christian View of Man* (New York: Charles Scribner's Sons, 1953), 148, 153.

dialogue between psychology and theology. It leads us to ask, "How has the dialogue between psychology and theology influenced our understanding of the human condition? What key insight has it produced in our perception of ourselves?" We ask such questions with a specific complex of concepts in mind, the theological concepts of sin, guilt, and forgiveness. Thus the question can be framed more precisely, "What has the dialogue between the two disciplines contributed to our understanding of humankind's plight and rescue?"

Although the authors in this book did not necessarily have this particular question in mind when they wrote, all of them are part of the modern scene in which psychological and theological understandings of the human condition have influenced one another. All of them take that dialogue seriously and in their own way contribute significantly to it.

Our study will be sequential. It will start with a consideration of sin, move through a discussion of guilt, and end with an explication of forgiveness. The sequence is not rigid, however, because the concepts themselves are intimately interrelated. Nevertheless, each section has its own unique focus.

The focus of the first section is on the integrity of the concept of sin in relation to the psychological concept of sickness. The authors represent a range of opinion on the issue—from Seward Hiltner's belief that psychological data are essential to a proper understanding of sin to J. Harold Ellens' idea that the concept of sickness is a corrective and complementary description of the human predicament.

Hiltner, one of the founding fathers of contemporary pastoral counseling, has been attentive to the relationship between psychology and theology. In chapter 1 he broadly defines the concept of sin to include the whole process of human brokenness from repentance to reparation. After clarifying how sin has been seen traditionally, he pursues his "unqualified conviction" that a psychological perspective "illuminates and clarifies our theological understanding of sin, and that what it critiques will be found to be deficient also from a theological point of view." Hiltner's assertion is radical. He maintains not only that psychology can increase our theological understanding. He also asserts that, as it uncovers human dynamics, it can critique our theologi-

cal beliefs and help determine their true meaning. Hiltner sup-
ports his contention by elaborating six ways in which psychology
contributes to a "better understanding" of sin.

In chapter 2, Ellens presents us with a psychospiritual view of
sin. He starts with the supposition that intense anxiety arising
from both threat and promise is generic to our human situation.
We tend to adopt either destructive or constructive mechanisms
to handle it. Destructive anxiety-reducing mechanisms lead to
distortion and pathology while constructive anxiety-reducing
mechanisms lead to the goal for which God created human life,
namely, fulfillment and wholeness. Ellens presents a fascinating
version of humankind's fall from his perspective. He notes factors that may have produced anxiety in Adam's and Eve's situation and makes a case for the belief that their story of anxiety and
wrong choice is our story.

Chapter 3 is a summary of the Second Calvinistic Conference
on Psychology and Psychiatry, which dealt with "The Place of the
Christian Conception of Sin in the Theory and Practice of Psychiatry." The account holds historical interest, but it is also significant because of the two positions represented.

Wendell Rooks, a psychiatrist, crosses the usual breach between sin and neurosis by setting forth a profound understanding
of sin as idolatry. Rooks maintains that idolatry is the basic
source of neurosis. He conceptualizes what he calls religiopsychological mechanisms that drive individuals toward death
when they are separated from, or rebel against, their Creator. We
may question his concept of "mechanisms," but his basic belief
that the whole person is out of whack when he or she is out of
relationship with God is theologically sound and pastorally heuristic. Ralph Heynen, a chaplain, deals with the "uneasy dialogue" between sin and sickness on John Calvin's premise that
life cannot be separated into isolated compartments. Heynen posits such a relationship between sin and sickness maintaining that
there is not one without the other. When he presses the relationship, though, he finds that in some cases (such as in neurosis) it is
difficult to tell whether an erratic behavior is a sin or a symptom.
Heynen seems to open the door for Menninger's concern about
sin. If it is a matter of choosing one or the other we may find that
symptom is the preferred explanation of human brokenness. Heynen avoids the trap by maintaining that each individual case must

be judged in terms of its own dynamics. He is less satisfying when he puts the matter as an "either/or," implying that if it is one it cannot be the other. In the final analysis he finds a significant gap between sin and sickness.

Ellens extends his consideration of sin in chapter 4. He asks if sin is a culture-bound term that is limited to certain ages or a more universal concept descriptive of the human predicament today. He distinguishes between two approaches to the human problem. The first approach, which Ellens calls a justice-justification model, operates on a praise-blame formula and makes God's mercy into a compensation for human failure. The second approach, a grace-discipline model, emphasizes growth and maturation as God's plan for us and it features unconditional care and empowerment whenever we fail to be what we are meant to be. Underneath Ellens' discussion is an intense search for a gracious God. He finds that God by maintaining that the metaphor of sickness contributes a constructive dimension to the metaphor of sin.

In chapter 5, Mowrer confronts us with two stark options of sin and sickness, an instinct theory that locates the root of illness in the repression of id impulses, and a moral theory that locates the root of illness in the repression of the superego. Mowrer represents the moral theory and tries to show that sickness is a direct result of unacknowledged sin and guilt. If that is true, the path to healing becomes theological—a path of public confession of sin and of proper restitution for it. Mowrer considers the possibility that sin may not be simply the cause of illness but that, in turn, illness may be an unconscious payment for sin. Although we may not agree with the whole of Mowrer's thought, we need to acknowledge that he raised crucial questions of psychology and pastoral care, and many of those questions are still relevant to our consideration of sin, guilt, and forgiveness.

John V. Gilmore, Jr., helps us to reflect on, and to critique, Mowrer's contentions. Gilmore affirms much in Mowrer's thought, including Mowrer's sensitivity to the role and importance of sin, guilt, and forgiveness in human brokenness and healing. He appreciates Mowrer's attempt to shift from a medical model to a moral model of human failure. Gilmore also makes it clear that he disagrees with the legalistic/moralistic orientation of Mowrer's psychotheological view of the human condition. Contrary to Mowrer, Gilmore is Pauline. He sees sin as the transgression of God's moral law and not just as the transgression of societal standards. In terms of guilt, this means our plight has to do with the absence of faith in God, and not just with a lost faith in our own conscience. Gilmore decries Mowrer's tendency to minimize confession to God over confession to peers. In terms of healing Gilmore chooses the reality and impact of God's forgiveness over any program of good works that seeks to motivate individuals to restore their health by their own efforts. Gilmore's conclusion is that Mowrer's position represents an "excessive scrupulosity" that is "more extreme than Pelagianism" and "that is not healthy psychologically."

Mowrer's and Gilmore's chapters serve as a transition into the second section of the book where the focus is on guilt. The discussion in this section is double-edged. On the one hand it deals with the need to clarify the nature of guilt, including its relation to shame, from both a psychological and a theological perspective; on the other hand it addresses the place of guilt in the human predicament and draws implications for our understanding of the task of psychotherapy and, more precisely, of pastoral care.

Chapter 7, taking clinical and theological considerations into account, distinguishes three types of guilt: "rule guilt" is the tangible transgression of social or religious laws; "existential guilt" is a violation of the self, the other, or the relationship between them; and "ultimate guilt" is sin against God which by its very nature is also inordinate self-elevation and unlimited desire to draw the surrounding world into the self. LeRoy Aden clarifies the interrelationship between the three levels of guilt and goes on to describe five experiential components of guilt that make it a heavy burden in the individual's personal, interpersonal, and spiritual life.

S. Bruce Narramore deals with several common misconceptions that lay Christians have about the origin and nature of guilt and uses a psychoanalytic perspective to arrive at a more adequate understanding. He reminds us that guilt is not a monolithic experience but an affective reaction "comprised of internalized fears of punishment, of rejection, and of loss of self-esteem." He identifies internal and external factors that are often responsible for guilt's arousal. He concludes by comparing the motivational value of guilt with the motivational value of love. He urges believers to return to the original insight of the Christian faith—that love, not guilt, encourages constructive change.

In chapter 9, Brad A. Binau presents an in-depth study of shame as a "possible experiential correlate to the law." From a psychological, biblical, and theological discussion of shame he lifts out the central finding that shame is the exposure, often the sudden and unwanted exposure, of misplaced trust. When interpreted in relational terms (as shame must be), his discovery means that shame is the exposure of our basic state of disrelationship. Law in contrast to gospel has this intent—to serve as a mirror in which we become aware of our brokenness, and in this sense shame is its "experiential correlate." Of particular interest is Binau's contention that baptism is a decisive Christian resource in helping people return to relationship.

People who feel unacceptable because of guilt try to make themselves acceptable to self, others, and God. As chapter 10 puts it, they engage in a life process of self-justification. The experience of pastoral counseling is that this attempt often involves suffering, denial, and tyrannical demands. These three endeavors of self-justification tend to aggravate rather than to resolve guilt. Counseling, especially pastoral counseling, should help the individual get beyond the compulsive concern to do something to a point where he or she can receive acceptance as an unearned gift.

If self-justification perpetuates the very guilt that it seeks to resolve, responsibility is a step out of it. Counselors have found that individuals can grow in their sense of responsibility. In fact, effective counseling promotes growth in a threefold sense: clients gain an increased ability to acknowledge their own faults, to exercise their freedom of self-determination, and to respond to situations in a fitting way. Each development is an important part of being responsible, but people move toward genuine fulfillment only when they are able to be responsible in the last sense.

LeRoy Aden's discussion of responsibility brings us to the third section of the book where the concern is forgiveness. The authors take a functional approach to forgiveness or, to put it in less abstract terms, they shed light on the way in which forgiveness is a living, empowering reality in human relationships. They give concrete richness to Tillich's observation that "nothing greater can happen to a human being than that he is forgiven."[6]

In chapter 14, E. Mansell Pattison distinguishes between punitive and reconciliation models of forgiveness. The former centers on the infraction of rules and requires punishment as a requisite to forgiveness; the latter deals with distorted or broken relationships and involves forgiveness given and received as requisite to reunion. Pattison's predilection is with the reconciliation model, but his primary attention is given to the punitive model, to the pathologies that interfere with the process of forgiveness. He reminds us that forgiveness, instead of being an answer to sin, can be used as an expression of it. He takes away our hiding places and forces us to stand before forgiveness as reconciliation.

Lyman T. Lundeen guides us on this path toward openness and reconciliation by setting forgiveness at the center of our life and our faith. This center is the juncture where a perspective of faith meets concrete human dynamics. His seven essential features of forgiveness cast a penetrating light on its nature and function. He shows that it opens up a vast new world of recreated relationships in which ideals are taken seriously, guilt is faced honestly, life's ambiguity is accepted willingly, and suffering for others is taken on voluntarily. He also shows that these things are possible, not only because God is the wellspring of forgiveness, but also because forgiveness assures us that we are dealing with a personal, gracious, and recreating God. "Your sins are forgiven" actualizes a new beginning—first with God and second, derivatively, with those from whom we are estranged.

Forgiveness heals families. With this simple assertion, Rinda G. Rogers brings an intergenerational perspective to bear on families to illuminate the basic way in which they become distorted and to clarify the pivotal way in which forgiveness serves as a healing agent. Families become unbalanced, repositories of unfair giving and receiving. Forgiveness redresses these relational injustices by being a dialogic act of turning toward, facing into, and rebuilding with others who share the same intergenerational space. Rogers concludes her study by suggesting that the church should teach the ritual aspects of forgiveness to families, so that

6. Paul Tillich, *The New Being* (New York: Charles Scribner's Sons, 1955), 7.

they might fulfill their God-ordained function of identity building.

In this book, sin, guilt, and forgiveness are taken off the theological shelf and placed in the middle of life. The authors do not claim to have exhausted the implications of the malady that besets us, but collectively they represent a variety of perspectives on it. They are serious about the dialogue between psychology and theology, and they use that dialogue to illuminate our plight and our rescue. Some of the insights are of enduring value, a few of them are of dated importance, but one thing is pivotal: Sin, guilt, and forgiveness become realities that are found not on the periphery of life but at its very center. They are concrete human dynamics, present in the lowliest aspects of our transient existence and operative in the highest reaches of our spiritual striving.

If sin, guilt, and forgiveness lie at the heart of the human predicament, they also are central to our therapeutic attempt to heal. And if they are to lie at the heart of our attempt to heal, they must first be part of our desire to be healed. They are the beginning and the end of any concretion of human wholeness.

The authors wish to acknowledge the work of Paul Ingram, assistant copy-editor at Baker Book House.

Sin

1

Sin: Theological and Psychological Perspectives

SEWARD HILTNER

With the knowledge and insight that the psychological disciplines have made available, especially in recent years, it is both legitimate and important to explore various questions about sin. No psychological perspective by itself, however, can provide an adequate conception of the phenomenon to be explored. That is available only in an explicit theological framework and context. It is necessary, therefore, to begin by summarizing what theology has meant by sin. With that established and distinguished from its distortions, psychological perspectives may be brought to bear freely upon it.[1]

Theological Perspective

Sin, like all other Christian teachings, appears within the context of the relation of human beings to God as Creator and Sustainer of all things, the original understanding stemming from the Jewish heritage of Christianity. According to that heritage, human beings were creatures of God and not, as some religions

1. A further discussion of sin can be found in Seward Hiltner, *Theological Dynamics* (Nashville: Abingdon, 1972).

23

have declared, pieces of or emanations of God. As creatures, human beings were held to share creaturely characteristics with some other forms of life that God made. Perhaps above all, they are bodies, and their bodiliness is not optional or dispensable equipment, but is basic to their being human.

At the same time they are bodily creatures, however, human beings are made in the image of God. As the crowning work of God's earthly creation, they have been endowed with capacities for both freedom and relatedness which, although far less than those of God, are much superior to those of other creatures—so much so that the phrase *made in the image of God* is relevant so long as "image" is understood to be a likeness or similarity rather than a complete mirror reflection or the product of a die stamp. Creaturely limitations and characteristics like those of God go together; they may be paradoxical but are not contradictory.

The ancient Hebrews declared further that, in some very basic sense, human beings were created with the capacity for using their freedom and their relatedness toward their optimal fulfillment, including their continuing awareness of him as their Creator and continuing Guide. For that basic capacity the traditional term was "original righteousness." The actual human situation, however, as the Jews looked upon it, was different. Freedom was being misused in massive ways, and relatedness had become either exploitation of other human beings or ignoring God. Whatever produced these distortions, it was not God, whose creation had been given original righteousness. The misuses were, therefore, clearly human productions; their start could be called "original sin."

It should be emphasized that the fall into sin was not produced by finitude or by creaturely limitation. The cause was not human mortality, or human ignorance, or human sexuality, or any other characteristic suggesting limitation. It was, instead, what we might now call some kind of cultivated distortion in the human psyche, viewed first collectively, then also individually. Nevertheless, the Jews connected finitude with sin. The original sin appeared when human creatureliness and finitude were denied rather than accepted, but something other than the finitude itself motivated the denial. That something was of human, not divine, origin.

From the point of view of the prophets and others who, all through the Old Testament, understood sin in this way, what was to be done about it? They declared two responses, one active and the other passive. First, sin was to be repented of, whether through the "acting out" of sacrificial rites in the early period or through the direct change of attitude in the later period. But such attitudinal shifts could not be permitted to serve as new occasions for sin, as if a button were pushed and then God had to do as requested. In his own way and time, God would reward genuine repentance if it led to optimal use of freedom and relatedness. But, second, God must be trusted about all this. Even a repentant Israel must wait upon the Lord, not use its repentance as a bargaining agent. Such an attitude must, if truly repentant, discard human time tables and detailed plans. Hope comes from faith in God's love. Even his wrath is a form of that love, but it is directed not against human beings but only against their sin.

When the geographical and social conditions of the Old Testament are recalled, it is understandable that the primary form in which sin was cast was rebellion. Whether in the earlier nomadic situation or the later agricultural way of life, the need for stability and order was put in great jeopardy by persons or groups who rebelled against the law and its executors. But the naturalness of the rebellion metaphor for that time and place does not, however, suggest it as necessarily the best way to understand sin in all times and places.

One final observation seems needed about sin before leaving the Old Testament, namely, the primarily social or collective character of sin. The largest architect of the time was the Tower of Babel Committee. Even though Aaron served for a time as executive of the Golden Idol Committee, it had lots of members. Even Samson's final undoing involved a group of two. The predominantly story form of the Old Testament, with its many villains and flawed heroes and heroines, should not obscure their representation of collectivities beyond themselves.

The basic meaning of sin, and the context in which it was understood, was not basically changed by the New Testament and the events that gave rise to it. The incarnation was not an admission by God that he had made a mistake in the original creation. In the sending of his son, however, to be fully human as we are and to suffer the consequences of not yielding to the collective power of sin, God was performing a culminating act of love. The ancient motif of sacrifice was honored for the final occasion as an act, and could henceforth become participative remembrance. Jesus' teaching, focused around the kingdom, showed that the power of sin could be broken now in principle (which means, as Tillich noted, "in power and beginning"), even though human plans and time tables about fulfillment must be laid aside while waiting upon the Lord. No longer could there be the excuse that God did not understand things from the human point of view or that human beings could find God inscrutable.

Christianity was the first world faith claiming exclusive allegiance that was not necessarily tied to race and soil and culture, for it came to the Greek as well as to the Jew. The most obvious consequence, therefore, was its claim upon individuals as well as groups, so that even members of families could be divided about accepting it. More significantly, however, the community of the church replaced the earlier kind of racial collectivity.

The positive part of the New Testament development was the provision of a new kind of community to nurture persons into repentance and then into mutual support and service against the power of sin. It was not necessary to go it alone or to wait until an entire people were ready. No legalistic efforts were needed for righteousness, only following in the way Jesus had shown. There could be a qualified optimism not only about the future but also about the present.

On the other side, the Christian teaching that God had become incarnate and had broken the power of sin once and for all carried the temptation to forget that only God can make time tables and detailed plans. The metaphor for sin of missing the mark is in part an illustration of this temptation. The analogy is of throwing a spear at a target, implying that missing by a little is as bad as missing by much. The metaphor is legitimate, but if there is a temptation to perfectionism the meaning of sin itself is distorted.

In summarizing the theological discussion of sin, we may note, first, the restricted sense in which sin is about blame. That sense is that sin comes from human misuse of capacities and not from God or his creation. In other senses, the critical word concerning sin is repentance; true acknowledgment of sin, with correspondingly appropriate change means that although sin is evil, the news of sin is good. They who genuinely repent have broken the power of sin, even though they do not thereby become sinless.

Second, precisely because the most basic form of sin is social and collective, only another kind of community, the church, can help the person to continue repenting of it and to avoid its occasions. Trying to go it alone is itself a prideful form of sin, for it denies the basic structure of human relatedness.

Third, although the early metaphors for understanding the nature of sin are still not without usefulness, any analogy that promotes genuine understanding is to be welcomed. Rebellion, especially conceived against an arbitrary ruler, will not do. But rebellion may still take the form of denying our creaturehood, trying to make God unnecessary, or trying to live, as Reinhold Niebuhr put it, as if one had conquered all his limitations.[2] In early Christian history the Greek word *hybris* was used to denote this kind of rebellious arrogance; and if that meaning is precisely retained, it may be argued that *hybris* is the root of all sin, even though not the sole way in which to see sin nor the sole form in which sin appears.

We saw that the analogy of missing the mark has the virtue of calling for the bull's eye on repentance, but it also carries the danger of perfectionism. Our Protestant heritage has especially alleged that there is no such thing as a little sin, that all sin is offensive to God and an obstacle to our proper fulfillment. Perhaps the sense in which this metaphor may be most meaningful today is in terms of settling for too little in life, of failing to cultivate our God-given talents, of failing to fulfill our lives by severe restrictions on our creativity. So understood, this could be similar to the form of sin that Niebuhr called "sensuality," by which he meant living under or beneath our limits.

The most popular metaphor for sin in recent years has been isolation or estrangement. The emphasis here is upon relatedness, or its absence, while both rebellion and missing the mark focus around misuse of freedom. Sin as estrangement is certainly a needed corrective. But the sin in estrangement is not basically subjective feelings of isolation, however terrorizing those may be;

---

2. Reinhold Niebuhr, *The Nature and Destiny of Man* (New York: Charles Scribner's Sons, 1941), vol. 1.

it is rather unawareness of the relatedness to God that God himself has bestowed both in his creation and in his consummate act of incarnation.

Thus, the person or group who experiences estrangement as sin will become aware of God and Jesus Christ, and thus be in the process of repenting. Granted the nature of God as revealed in Jesus Christ, the estrangement is a subjective barrier that true repentance can alter.

Fourth, we may need Paul's reminder that sin is never to be understood in terms of isolated acts, but appears when certain forms of readiness to act in certain ways have been cultivated, if only by inattention to alternatives. The works of the flesh (*sarx* and not *sōma* or body) cited by Paul are dispositions to act habitually in particular ways. It is they that stand in opposition to the fruits of the Spirit like love, joy, and peace. If I remember my Latin correctly, Thomas's use of *actus* in relation to sin did not necessarily mean an overt, observable act. Such acts could demonstrate sin, for there would be something behind them. But an *actus* could be taking place even without external signs at all. Such a view is more than a behaviorism—at least in the common sense of the term.

Fifth, it is time that Protestants begin to understand that some typology of sin is necessary, and that it is possible without falling back into the casuistry that caused them earlier to dispense altogether with acknowledged typologies of all kinds. I would of course uphold those ancestors who regarded any sin as heinous and ultimately self-destructive, not permitting so-called little or venial sins to pass by without much notice. As will be argued later, however, some forms of sin lead more inexorably to irreversible consequences than others. Hence, even though the older typologies of Catholicism will not do, they should be succeeded by improved typologies, not by none at all, nor by surreptitiousness and uncriticized typologies to which Protestantism has resorted in actual practice.

Psychological Perspective

The early modern explorers in depth psychology, especially for therapeutic purposes, discovered that the incapacitating feelings of guilt they encountered tended to be misplaced, were not really about what they appeared to be, and could be dealt with only by tracing their origin and development in psychic and inter-personal life. The less cautious among them probably gave the impression that all feelings of guilt were displacements to be eliminated. A few of them incautiously used the word *sin* as a synonym for such feelings, thus implying the desirability of out-growing the notion of sin.

Theological defenders of the faith interpreted such reflections as attacks upon the nature of the Christian teaching that human beings are objectively sinful before God. They drew the battle line as the defense of objectivity against what they believed to be the wholly subjectivizing tendency of psychology. In doing so, they tended to overlook the contribution the early depth psychologists were making to distinguishing misplaced feelings of guilt from actual guilt, a distinction psychologists themselves eventually took more seriously, especially when their concerns moved from conscience-ridden psychoneurotic sufferers to psychopathic and sociopathic persons appearing to have no conscience at all.

The apologists also tended to forget some aspects of their theo-logical heritage on sin. For instance, if repentance of sin is genu-ine, and the feelings of guilt focused where they should, then those feelings should be dissipated as the good news about grace through Jesus Christ is assimilated. Thus, even theologically, the perpetuation of guilt feelings, with no sort of resolution, clearly called into question the genuineness of the repentance. The early modern psychologists might indeed misunderstand the meaning of sin and its proper context, but their error hardly justified theo-logians in distorting aspects of their heritage.

Unhappily, the discussion of the possible contribution of the dynamic psychologies to understanding theological teaching has continued to focus on the subjectivity/objectivity question. No doubt this tendency has received renewed provocation from the brashness of some psychologists who became entangled in a "nothing but" form of metaphysics. But the fact is that the real issues do not lie at this point. If the analysis of subjectivity is pursued far enough and with competence, it is bound to acknowl-edge realities that are not themselves mere subjectivities, even if the restriction of these to a kind of "psychological ontology" is as strong as it is, for instance, in Jung.

Some early modern theological apologists, impressed with the practical usefulness of the dynamic psychologies, attempted to domesticate those for theological use while tabling any exploration of the possible use of psychology to critique and illuminate basic theological teachings. It is probable that this tendency has been reinforced by the generally pragmatic character of the American people. Important and valuable as the modern movement for improved pastoral care has been, it has tended generally to take this line, making practical use of certain findings of the dynamic psychologies but tabling the question about basic relationships.

Tabling the basic issues, however, will not do. In the remainder of this discussion a limited number of suggestions will be made about how psychological perspectives may contribute to a better understanding of our focal topic, sin, when the concept itself is viewed in the way set forth by the best in our theological heritage. It is my unqualified conviction that this procedure clarifies our theological understanding of sin and that what it critiques will be found to be deficient, also from a theological point of view. Six potential contributions will be noted, though they are far from being exhaustive.

First, a psychological perspective gives promise of unraveling the complex question of the extent to which conscious awareness of wrongdoing or violation is an essential ingredient of sin. There have always been some legalists holding, as does much civil and criminal law, that ignorance or unawareness is no excuse. But Thomas in particular, and most of Protestantism and Catholicism in general, have held that actions undertaken in genuine ignorance, while they may produce evil, are not sinful.

Now that psychology has revealed the complexities about awareness, including many degrees and nuances, it becomes possible to redefine the question. One way to do this is to ask to what extent the person or group has "complicity" in what it has done. For instance, if racial prejudice is inculcated in a person or group by the surrounding culture, the "original sin" is found in that culture rather than in the person or small group as such. But since other views and factors would also, in the modern world, impinge upon the person or group, there would have to be "complicity" in the main cultural pattern if the prejudice is to be perpetuated. No matter how complex the actual psychic processes involved, the actual sin as related to person or group would be detected by the degree of complicity. This way of viewing the question appears superior to the old way, partly because the question can then be explored in operational terms and partly because the call to repentance can be more discriminating.

With this kind of approach, sin can take on a more appropriate diagnostic character, and some issues about wilfulness versus victimization can be transcended. The deprived adolescent reared in the slums and the suburban teenager reared without genuine affection can be understood as predominantly victims, while at the same time the necessity for both to be supported in moving beyond their handicaps, rather than in using them as justification, can be affirmed. It can become clearer that blame is relevant to sin only at the general point that sin is a human production, not a creation of God, and that God's concern is to free human beings from the power of sin rather than to assign degrees of blame. Except in the context of grace, sin has no meaning.

A second contribution of a psychological perspective is to show the sense in which the collective form of sin is prior to the individual, yet the individual has responsibility that cannot be evaded by reference to the collective. We have all worked with people who could more easily admit flaws in themselves, for instance, than in a parent. We have understood that when they attain a clearer view of the parent, it is important that their sense of responsibility for their own lives is increased rather than decreased.

A psychological perspective can also help clarify the basic function that the church should perform in the lives of persons. As the primary temptations to sin come from one kind of collectivity, it is essential that another kind of collectivity operate to guide, induce repentance, and engage in continuing proclamation of the means of grace. Humanly fallible as all existing churches are, they are also the principal agents of grace, and the divinely instituted church does somehow operate amid the collective flaws and sins of the church as human institution. Shaded glens and singing birds are not substitutes for church. This insight becomes peculiarly important in a day when even many faithful church participants regard the church condescendingly as optional equipment, or as merely incidental to their pursuit of the Christian life.

Third, a psychological perspective can help to clarify the basic relationship between sin and repentance on the one side and forgiveness, grace, justification, and *metanoia* on the other. To guard against any possible reliance on works as ways to salvation, the Protestant reformers declared that justification is by grace through faith alone. In guarding against the danger of a wrong kind of self-dependence, this declaration of the Reformers is no less valid today than it was in the sixteenth century. But it was not then, and is not now, a reliable picture of what goes on in psychic life when there is genuine repentance of sin and the acceptance of divine forgiveness.

A psychological perspective suggests that the process is more dialectical than the Reformers thought. Trying to use more neutral terms in his exploration of these processes, Joseph Havens spoke of the sense of "self-power" and the sense of "other-power"; and he found a kind of alternation of these two when he studied the journal of an early American Quaker, Stephen Grellet, who was even more revealing in some aspects than John Woolman.[3] In the material available about Martin Luther, Havens found a similar alternation, which enabled him to avoid contradiction between the forceful and aggressive side of Luther and the other side that really did wait on grace and was aware of continuing sinfulness. The work of Havens has been a good start, but far more is needed on this question.

Fourth, a psychological perspective can help with the metaphors or analogies by which we may grasp the basic meaning of sin. Rebellion, the earliest metaphor, may now be understood not only in relation to agencies outside the self but also against unintegrated dimensions of the self. In addition, with the modern insight that the dynamics of rebellion and conformity are similar, extreme conformity can be seen to have the same motivating factors as extreme rebellion. Whether in rebellion or conformity, it is quite possible that the object is both outside and inside at the same time.

It has already been suggested that the metaphor of isolation or estrangement has appeal for the modern mind but not always for the right reason. If one feels isolated and interprets his predicament as victimization, no room is left for confessing one's complicity in the estrangement, yet the latter is required if isolation is

---

3. Joseph D. Havens, "Psychotherapy and Salvation," (Ph.D. diss., University of Chicago, 1956).

to be a way of understanding sin. What a psychological perspective can do is to show the complex causes of the estrangement, both outside and inside the self, including the self's complicity. But isolation as victimization from outside, or from God or fate, is not about the complexities of the relationship between collective and individual sin.

Other metaphors have appeared in both theological and secular thought which may help to clarify the meaning of sin. Yet we must be cautious that any metaphor distort that meaning. The web, for instance, offers the legitimate notion of being caught and unable to extricate the self. But it can also lend itself to the idea that one is simply a victim, which is false.

Ever since William James, the notion of the divided self has had widespread appeal, and in more recent years it has been regarded as the opposite of integrity or integration of the personality.[4] An extreme form of integrity theory may be found in Abraham Maslow and Carl Rogers, where the ultimate "bad guy" seems to be culture inhibiting both self-development and self-integration.[5] However unconsciously, such views usually rest metaphysically on an oversimplified monism; and, although they may take evil seriously, they tend to regard it as an imposition upon the self. There is a lack of complicity in the real self. It would seem that any "divided self" metaphor for sin must have the self assume responsibility, at least through complicity, for its division.

Although Karl Menninger does not offer constructive new metaphors for understanding sin, he performs an important service at this point by warning against what he regards as some of the incorrect analogies that have almost caused the notion of sin to disappear.[6] He argues, for instance, that sin cannot be collapsed into crime, into symptoms, or into a kind of "collective irresponsibility" that appears to leave our own hands clean. Menninger does not, however, explore actual therapeutic processes for their possible contribution to metaphors clarifying the

4. William James, *The Varieties of Religious Experience* (Cambridge, Mass.: Harvard University Press, 1985).
5. See, for example, Abraham Maslow, *Toward a Psychology of Being* (Princeton: Van Nostrand, 1968); Carl R. Rogers, *Person to Person* (Lafayette, Calif.: Real People, 1967); Carl Rogers, *Carl Rogers on Encounter Groups* (New York: Harper and Row, 1970).
6. Karl Menninger, *Whatever Became of Sin?* (New York: Hawthorn, 1973).

meaning of sin. This latter would appear to be potentially fruitful.

We may think, for instance, of the distrustful person who, in spite of repeated genuine efforts on our part, continues to deny that we have genuine concern for him. And then, on some occasion, events compel him to acknowledge that we really care. Briefly, there is then a sense of relief, release, and even exaltation. But quickly our very concern appears to lay new burdens upon the person. His old excuse, "Nobody cares," can no longer be used. His partial acceptance of our genuine concern compels him to move toward new levels of self-responsibility; his subjective feelings, at least for a time, are more negative than when he had his security blanket. Subtle as this is, it might be stated in such a way as to show how the complicity element in sin moves the person away from precisely that resource that can help disarm its power.

Fifth, a psychological perspective may help in clarifying the relationship between acts, in the ordinary sense, and habituated readinesses. In his interview with reporters from *Playboy* magazine during his campaign for the presidency, Jimmy Carter tried to be honest, noting that we have all had lust in our eye even if we have not engaged in adulterous behavior. The wide variety of responses to his statement suggested that widespread bias, misinformation, and general confusion still reigns in this whole area.

If sin is not simple isolated acts but *actus* in the plural set off by habituated readiness, then it becomes clear that sin has the best chance of remaining untouched if the readinesses that trigger it can be regarded as untouchable because the culture approves them or at least does not disapprove them. If there is to be repentance of sin, it is equally clear, it is the readinesses and the implicit cultural approval behind them that have to be exposed and understood for what they are. Disapprobation of behavior or even penalties for it under some conditions are not enough. Because this is true, the exposure of sin in many realms of life is impossible without considerable knowledge of that field or kind of situation. Thus the agent who would convict people of sin in the theological sense in any particular area of life must be convincing in his knowledge of that area. He must also, of course, in modern language, come in on the side of the ego, and not be experienced as enemy.

Finally, a psychological perspective may help in constructing typologies of sin which do not deny the evil in any sin but which distinguish between degrees of irreversibility according to the forms of sin. Certainly there is a probable difference in consequences for the user of opium products as against the smoker of marijuana. Not all sexual behaviors of the same general kind, even among those regarded as morally wrong by either civil or church law, lead to the same serious consequences.

Perhaps the clue that a psychological perspective may use in the direction of such a typology can be taken from Niebuhr.[7] More clearly than anyone else in our time, he showed that the greatest potential for evil through sin appears precisely when the self becomes most self-transcendent or free. It may be precisely after we have helped a person successfully that this form of sin acquires the greatest potential for evil, not during the painful counseling process when conflict and psychic pain limit the kind of harm the self might do. For such development, however, both psychologists and theologians will have to move beyond preoccupation with immediate successful outcomes and realize that these are moments of beginning, rather than of end.

7. Niebuhr, *Nature and Destiny*.

2

A Psychospiritual View of Sin

J. HAROLD ELLENS

Since humans first sensed the radical and generic nature of their spiritual and psychological fallenness, the most essential and universal human experience has been that of anxiety. Generic human anxiety is both systemic and situational to the human person. It is so radical in nature, that is, so close to the essence of human identity, that everything human is in some dimension shaped by it. Erich Fromm adequately describes the tragic side of its impact in human affairs in his book *The Anatomy of Human Destructiveness*.[1] John G. Finch has argued with considerable effect that generic human anxiety is also a potentially constructive dynamic in human growth.[2] Seward Hiltner has effectively related human anxiety and divine grace.[3] Barbara Mertz relates generic human anxiety to both our terror and our hope.[4]

1. Erich Fromm, *The Anatomy of Human Destructiveness* (New York: Holt, Rinehart, and Winston, 1973).
2. John G. Finch, "The Message of Anxiety" (taped lecture, Christian Association for Psychological Studies convention, 1976).
3. Seward Hiltner and Karl Menninger, eds., *Constructive Aspects of Anxiety* (Nashville: Abingdon, 1963).
4. Barbara Mertz, *Red Land, Black Land* (New York: Coward-McCann, 1966).

36

Our Terror

The terror dimension of anxiety is readily identified by and in all humans. It ranges broadly from our struggle to come to terms with death and our omnipresent mortality to such forms of exaggerated anxiety as those that are usually identified as, or produce, the plethora of pathologies we clinically speak of as neuroses. From the moment that uterine contractions signal impending birth until the last gasp of life's breath in enfeebled old age, life offers an overarching set of anxiety-inducing threats to stasis, to goal achievement, to fulfillment, and to vital existence itself. The whole spectrum of life's experience process may be comprehensively and definitely described as a conscious and subconscious endeavor aimed at gaining control of one's destiny.

The native sense of psychological and spiritual fallenness universal to humans is surely rooted in that initial loss of the paradisiacal world of the womb, in which security is normally the overriding quality of experience. That loss is not experienced benignly. It engrains in our earliest and most essential precognitive, psychospiritual experience a sense of the essential violent and tragic character of life. That humans ever achieve any genuine stasis and functionality after the birth trauma is really quite surprising and is evidence of the divine gift of the resilient force of life and will.[5] The beginning of terrors is really the experience of being torn violently and painfully from that setting to which we are adjusted, even committed. It is a place we love systemically in the sense that we are identified with, attached to, and dependent on it. Birth, therefore, means the loss experience not merely of separation, but of separation perceived as alienation. That alienation is experienced in conjunction with an overwhelming sense of fragility, vulnerability, and disenfranchisement. In terms of the classic dynamics of grief, that vulnerability is probably interpreted by the precognitive neonate as unworthiness. Our alienation from God and the godly, personally and as a community, reinforces all this sense.

In summary, our common human terror is that of being wrenched from our mother's womb and being unable to catch hold of our father's hand. The essential psychological and spiri-

5. Rollo May, *Love and Will* (New York: W. W. Norton, 1969).

tual experience is that of being orphaned. As is the case with children who experience pain and grief-loss, we internalize that sense of lostness, personally and communally, as guilt. That guilt ultimately produces anger, because the rationality of that guilt is almost impossible to identify, and the anger reinforces our sense of alienation, producing our psychological and spiritual depression, distortions, pathologies, and hostile, inappropriate behavior. Here lies the threat of the loss of hope and of the meaningfulness and worthwhileness of things; here is the engine driving our sin.

Our Hope

On the other hand, the separation experience of birth, as well as that of adolescent disengagement, brings with it the promise of hope. Both are pregnant with new possibilities. Birth brings a new breath of fresh air, as does the adolescent-young adult adjustment process and growth. In this the ontogeny of the person, so to speak, recapitulates the phylogeny of the cosmos.

Both the creation and the fall were oriented toward the future; both were driven by the dynamics of expectation; both were filled with the potential of new life and a new world. The first was paradisiacal, the second, tragic, but in a certain fundamental sense, both were part of the birth process of the universe. Both reached for the denouement of salvation and the completion and resolution of all things. Creation, fall, and redemption comprise a historical paradigm of the universal human psychodynamic process of womb tranquility, birth trauma, adolescent disengagement, and maturation.[6] As in the paradigm, so in the psychology of the development of persons, the trauma of our genesis and the pain and risks of adolescence are drawn together into a comprehensive birth process from which the person comes, reaching consciously and subconsciously for the denouement of health and maturity with its healing resolution of things and its closures.

Health and maturation, which can be comprehended in such terms as "healing" and "wholeness," are achieved by stages, in fits and starts, with distortions, regressions and pathologies,

6. C. Markham Berry, "Entering Canaan: Adolescence as a Stage of Spiritual Growth," *Bulletin of CAPS* 6, 4 (1980): 10–13.

hopeful surges and dead-end streets. The whole process reaches hopefully forward expecting fulfillment of the total potential of wholeness inherent in God's image-bearers and in God's cosmic experiment.

The whole of life and history, therefore, can be described as the process of trauma moving toward hope, tragedy driving to denouement, pained and distorted life reaching for wholeness, anxiety wanting reduction, dissonance longing for resolution.

Since the whole process of personal and cosmic function moves from incompleteness and pathology (lostness, distortion, and palpable illness) to maturity and wholeness (health, fulfillment, and palpable salvation), the efficiency with which this is accomplished depends directly upon the effectiveness of the reduction of distorting obstructions. In the biblical historical paradigm for the cosmos and the human community, the reduction of obstructions has to do with the removal of the bonds of chaos in Genesis 1:1, of primitivity and naiveté in Genesis 1 and 2, and of idolatry in the rest of Scripture. In the individualized psychodynamic odyssey of each person, the reduction of obstructions to wholeness involves anxiety reduction and thus transcendence over the pathology and distortions anxiety brings. Incidentally, in both the historical cosmic quest and the individual odyssey, wholeness is achieved ultimately *sola gratia* but not *soli Deo gloria*. Because grace is grace the wholeness that it brings is, through incarnation, for the creation. History, the Bible, and sound psychotherapy are in that sense human-centered. God, theology, and Christian psychology, when authentically perceived and expressed, are for and preoccupied with suffering persons and a suffering world (worlds).

Anxiety-reduction processes in the odyssey of personal growth may, of course, be constructive or destructive. I am convinced that all distortions, pathologies, and dead-end streets (self-destructive courses) in human psychospiritual development are the consequences of destructive anxiety-reduction mechanisms at the level of the psyche or at the level of social function, or both. Conversely, wholesome growth, health, and maturation are achieved to the degree that constructive anxiety-reduction mechanisms are introduced and utilized.

Destructive anxiety-reduction mechanisms are those that produce inhibitory defense processes in human growth. Constructive anxiety-reduction mechanisms are those that enhance the openness for assertive risk-taking processes in human growth. Destructive anxiety-reduction mechanisms obstruct, delay, distort, limit, or sicken and thus prevent the efficient move toward total self-actualization as an image-bearer of God whose destiny it is to realize palpable fulfillment of the psychospiritual potential. Constructive anxiety-reduction mechanisms support, direct, reinforce, equip, embellish, and expand the human person and thus promote the efficient move toward total self-actualization. That realization of human destiny as the fulfillment of the full range of the psychospiritual potential with which God has invested us is the very definition of health and wholeness. Every function or behavior designed to bring that about is a healing act and the very definition of healing. All our sinfulness and our sickness is thus a falling short of the glory of God, because it is an obstruction of his glorious ambition for us: a falling short of the glory of real humanness. We can elaborate this point in terms of the Genesis account of the fall of humankind.

Psychodynamics of the Fall

The story of the fall of human beings into the sin of prideful disobedience recorded in the Bible provokes a spontaneous and universal sense of its authenticity. It is one of those stories that carries with it such archetypical quality that we sense at once that it touches, at the center, a generic truth of obvious human history and of vital personal experience. It speaks of the radical tragic distance between what we can imagine as our paradisiacal potential as persons and what we know as our often defeating and dissonant experience in real life.

The Function of the Story

One major reason for the inclusion of the fall story in Scripture seems to be to establish a base line for dealing with the problem of evil as humans suffer it. The claim is unquestionably that a hubristic egotism led humans beyond their appropriate domain and landed them in such an erroneous perspective that God's design for nature, for communion, and for human relations seemed alien. The flowering shrubs began to look like thorns, the walks with God began to look like threat, and the complexity of relationship began to look like a thicket of unsortable confusion and pain.

The fall story endeavors to account for the problem of human pain and universal disorder. It attempts to explain why humans can conceive of aesthetic ideals but not create them, can long for a perfect world but not fashion one, can hope for genuine love but seldom express or experience it, can remember and anticipate Paradise yet sense it eluding us.

It is an intensely pathetic story of loss, grief, guilt, and shame. The pathos of the story is equally significant in revealing the essential nature of the universal human predicament. The truth it articulates is that of the general state of fallenness humans universally experience, expressed in the pervading distortion, debilitating anxiety, and apparent wrongness of human existence.

If one takes the story of the fall seriously as an element in a cosmic paradigm for general human psychological development, it becomes a crucial stage in human growth from the childlikeness of Eden to mature kingdom building and cultural responsibility. In that growth process, the story plays a role that has equivalents in the human growth process of birth and adolescent disengagement. Those personal separation processes are normally fraught with significant anxiety. Such anxiety is also evident in the reaction of Adam and Eve to events. There is significant anxiety with regard to the presence of the forbidden tree, to the perception of the possibility of making a forbidden decision, to the appearance of the tempting serpent, to the offer of the seduction of Eve, to her offer of seduction to Adam, to the threat of death, and to the guilt and shame of cutting loose from God. The whole fabric expresses intense anxiety.

The most interesting element is the plain implication of a significant and dangerous state of anxiety existing in the life and spirit of Adam and Eve before the fall, when Paradise was still intact. The recognition of significant anxiety before the fall is crucial for insight into essential human nature as seen by the Hebrews. It implies the need in Adam, as he was created, for an anxiety-reduction mechanism that would make it possible for him to cope and to open up the door of his primitive and childlike life to real growth in terms of his God-given potential as a person with a growth-oriented destiny. As soon as God announced the presence and import of the forbidden tree, a state of anxiety existed in terms of Adam's perception that his potential destiny was open-ended and required decision making by him and Eve. He recognized that he possessed the potential for change and for negative or positive growth. The anxiety increases in intensity as the story recounts Adam and Eve struggling with the essential decision about their unknown and challenging future. The pressure of that anxiety is further increased as they contemplate, quite correctly, the possibility of being like God, knowing both good and evil.

It should not surprise us that the story describes Eden as anxiety laden. Stress in the prefall state is evident much earlier. Adam is described as finding himself alone in the garden in a state of sufficient disequilibrium that he looked for a mate or companion among the animals. He found none adequate or appropriate. God noted the stress and anxiety and intervened by creating Eve as a help appropriate to his neediness. Obviously she met some condition of lack and anguish in Adam and thereby reduced his stress and anxiety.

One can imagine that Adam had considerable stress from numerous directions in Eden: from the pressure of responsibility to keep the garden, to find companionship that was appropriate, to name the animals, to fashion a meaningful relationship with his wife, who ultimately chose a liberation course of independence and then seduced him into following her, presumably lest he lose her, and responsibility to obey and love God in a world where the manner of doing so held some ambiguity. The man was under pressure. His anxiety is not the consequence of his sin. His anxiety is clearly the consequence of his being a person with unexplored potential and possibilities. It is inherent to his nature and all human nature. It is inevitable to human existence, because of the nature of the potential for growth and the unfolding unknown that growth constitutes. The Hebrews saw that and related it to the potential in the world for the problem of evil. The fall story so precisely captures a truth generic to our existence that when we read the story five or six thousand years later or more, we find it touching the center of our predicament in some fundamental ways.

The story urges that all this stress and anxiety that Adam experienced culminated in the enigma of what to do about the possibility of being like God. The story of the fall describes the event and its decision as Adam's anxiety-reduction mechanism designed to free his psyche for further function, coping, and growth. The critical question, therefore, must be raised as to whether the event was a constructive or destructive anxiety-reduction mechanism for Adam and the human race. We ask the same question when we consider whether the painful process of birth and of adolescent disengagement is a constructive or destructive anxiety-reduction mechanism. It is important, because it will give us some clues as to whether we are to look at human alienation, pain, and anxiety and its consequences as difficult but inevitable stages in the evolution of persons and the human race or as an unfortunate aberration of a sinful or, at least, a destructive type.

Constructive or Destructive

If adolescent differentiation is seen as paradigmatic of the fall story or vice versa, it is useful to ask whether Adam might have done it any better way. Does humanity need to express so much disjunction and experience so much alienation and loss to achieve personhood and growth? Was it a constructive or a destructive anxiety-reduction mechanism?

It is tempting to say that Adam chose the best course and, in view of his limited knowledge and experience, the only one he really had available. That is a way of saying that the loss and alienation we all experience from the loss of the womb and the adolescent individuation, together with the distortion in the intrapsychic and psychosocial world that drives our sickness and our sin, is virtually inevitable. As we grow, our limited knowledge, experience, and wisdom prevent us from choosing other than the painful and, at least temporarily, alienating course. Such a hypothesis would manage most of the relevant data neatly. This hypothesis implies that pain was inevitable, that the choice could not have been different if growth and maturation were to evolve out of the primitive and childlike naiveté of the Eden womb.

It is clear, however that the overall message of the fall story is that humanity made a bad choice. That does not imply that some decisive act by Adam to move him from naiveté to maturity was not necessary. Neither does it mean that nothing constructive toward real growth came out of Adam's decision. It only contends that his decision was a transitional act unnecessarily fraught with self-defeating pride, rebellion, and alienation.

If one posits the notion that the fall story represents a destructive anxiety-reduction mechanism for Adam and, paradigmatically, represents the disorder and alienation in humans as an essentially destructive and self-defeating response to the generic anxiety of birth and differentiation, that does not erase the fact that the fall has constructive, freedom-affording results for humans. Similarly, adolescence may be handled unnecessarily rebelliously by some teen-agers but lead to growth that results in profoundly healthy relationships with parents, authorities, and traditions later on. Paul seems to imply something of this regarding humanity when he ties the primordial state of human "bliss" into a continuum with "fallen man" and the fruition of it all in the "new person in Christ."

The fall story represents one option for implementing the necessary and inevitable differentiation process. Presenting it as a destructive option, the implication is that Adam might have exercised an equally growth-inducing act of will and ego strength by choosing, for independent and personal reasons, to affirm God's will and value system. That would have been as initiatory, independent, disengaging an act toward growth as disobedience proved to be. Presumably it would, moreover, have had less self-defeating, though adequately self-affirming, consequences. Moreover, the paradigmatic import for human history is the implication that the distortion, pain, alienation, and sickness with which humans have responded to generic anxiety through history were not inevitable elements of the growth process of the race. Humans have made many bad decisions in the way they have apprehended God's real disposition toward them, in the way they have responded to quandary and ambiguity, and in the finesse with which they have affected their own psychological dynamics and destiny. Such decisions can be made wisely, redemptively, and faithfully, with healthier consequences.

Paradigmatically, the disengaging adolescent can achieve health and growth while choosing, as an independent act of will and ego, to affirm and follow the healthful values of parents, authority, tradition, or other sources of encouragement toward conformity. Indeed that course, when expressing rather than compromising the child's own authenticity, may be far less self-defeating, inefficient, damaging to health, and painful than dis-engagement that strains relationships or maximizes confrontation, alienation, and grief-loss.

The story of the fall confesses the meaning of human pain and disorder in the face of a gracious and provident God who generously created and sustains us. Seward Hiltner contends that the story of the fall is a metaphor of the human process of maturing to individuality and to responsible agency as a person. He is correct in emphasizing the inevitable necessity of differentiation of human persons as persons from a womblike relation with God. It appears that the Hebrews were correct in implying that the disengagement could be less self-defeating and could affirm the perspective and value system that heals, rather than aggravates, generic human anxiety and so sickens us. Perhaps Howard J. Clinebell is really on the right track in deemphasizing the cataclysmic and alienating dimensions of human fallenness while placing all the emphasis on the freedom for growth that humans as independent agents need and possess. His model handles the data in a way that implies that the fall speaks of a revolution. However paradigmatic that may be of actual human experience, humankind has the option of evolutionary growth response to generic human anxiety.

It is intriguing to consider the possibility of humanity in general, and children in particular, developing through a peaceful, relatively nonturbulent exploration of the possibilities for being like God/parents, knowing good and evil.

My initial perspective in wrestling with the fall story in relationship to God's grace and human health was to conclude that Adam had no alternative. I was strongly inclined to the notion that turbulence and alienation are inherent to adolescence and its disengagement as well as to birth. Adam's action seemed to me to be the only constructive anxiety-reduction mechanism he had available to free him toward health and growth.

I am indebted to my daughter, Deborah Lynn, for forcing me to rethink that. The idea at the center of this chapter is really her argument that the fall story represents an unnecessary, self-destructive form of adolescent rebellion. Presumably Adam's growth and differentiation could have developed tranquilly and evolved constructively to maturity, as in healthy and cherishing adolescents. That seems clearly to be what the Hebrews intended to say.

It is intriguing, in any case, to contemplate how things might have been in human history if the state of affairs in the human psyche and spirit were such as to permit and prompt a different story in Genesis 3. What if the story could have represented humanity as reaching forward within the will of God, for individuality, maturity, and wisdom, and for knowledge of being like God in comprehending the world inside out, in knowing God as he now knows us? Cooperative growth with God and exploration of the possibilities of human destiny in tranquility is not a story that rings true to the human experience of dissonance, alienation, and dis-ease, but suggests a redemptive alternative that might have been from the beginning, if we were not so badly distorted by generic anxiety. It seems apparent that the invitation of grace to move into the growth mode of that redemptive option is really the whole issue of God's grace and human health.

God Imagers and the Fall

If we think of the fall and of human distortion as destructive anxiety-reduction dynamics, a final significant question regarding human nature arises. In what sense do humans image God in choosing self-destructive or self-defeating courses?

The human behavior of will and ego over a power and authority reflects, and is possible because of, an essential dimension of God's nature in humans: the function and attribute of being independent creators and independent agents of our own destiny. In the story of the fall and in the real human experience of pain, disorder, distortion, and dis-ease, humans act as independent creators gone awry and as independent agents choosing self-defeating destinies. Those choices free humans to be persons and to grow, but they decrease the focus, efficiency, and gratification of that freedom and increase the dissonance, conflict, and errosive sense of alienation.

God, as independent agent, could also act in self-defeating ways but does not. That is a credit to God's moral character as an independent moral being, not a result of his essential nature, as if he had no alternative.

Can God create a rock that is so heavy he cannot lift it? The question has greatly entertained the superficial and cynical secularist, and unduly troubled the Christian philosopher. It is to the credit of the superficial Christian and the secular philosopher, perhaps, that it troubled neither of them much, both thinking it quite absurd.

It is, however, a profound question. The answer is not the one that Christian philosophers have given, that is, that God cannot create a rock too heavy for God to lift since that is out of keeping with God's true character. The answer, I judge, is rather that God can very well create such a rock. He can do anything like that and any other sort of self-defeating thing, if he chooses to do so. Moreover, he can do it without ceasing to be God, contrary to the view of Christian philosophers. He would, of course, turn out to be a "bad" God in the moral sense of that term as well as in the social sense of the term. But he would not be a bad God in the ontological sense. He would still be God, and that is all that counts ontologically. In that sense it is not different for God than for humans who are bad morally and socially because they choose self-defeating behavior but remain humans in every ontological sense.

The crucial issue is that God has not created a rock too heavy for God to lift, so to speak, and has chosen not to engage in other self-defeating behavior because he has chosen to behave with inviolate moral integrity. He has chosen to be true to his own nature and destiny. He is not merely locked into an inevitable moral quality because of his essence. He is free to choose, grow, explore, experiment, decide, and fail.

He has chosen not to do so, not because of his essence, but because of his moral integrity and therefore, since all morality is ultimately aesthetics, because of his aesthetic integrity and sensitivity that cause his decision against self-defeating behavior. That is a matter of appropriateness and proportion. He is trustworthy, not merely as a being defined by logical or ontological inevitability, but as a being who is psychologically committed to holiness. Yahweh is not a Greek god in a pantheon of abstract qualities personified in archetypical figures. Yahweh is the Hebrew God, who chooses, acts, could err as Jesus could have at the temptation, and who decides not to do so. Yahweh decides to be moral, gracious, and sensitive.

Humans image God in the integrity of their choice processes. In that we are independent choosers, we image God and reflect his nature. We spoil the clear quality of the image when we

choose inappropriateness and disproportion and defeat ourselves in our growth endeavors or needs.

Such was the case in the fall. Such is the case in our daily
failures to make sound, wholesome, and healing choices. Humans
recapitulate the fall daily. That is undoubtedly why we so sponta-
neously perceive the authenticity of that ancient myth.

3

Sin and Sickness
in Clinical Practice

WENDELL ROOKS and RALPH HEYNEN

A Psychiatrist's Understanding of Sin:
Wendell Rooks

Man and woman were created in the image of God. This means that they were creatures with the ability to know God, to love God, and to find comfort in living in the right creature–Creator relationship. They were endowed psychologically with those mechanisms that enabled them to choose the right relationship. They would live if they did and die if they did not. They wanted omniscience and omnipotence. They refused to accept the divine condition and rebelled against their creature status. By choosing to be as God they denied the essential deity of a sovereign God, and set in motion those mechanisms that would eventually lead to death.

This chapter is taken from the Proceedings of the Second Calvinistic Conference on Psychology and Psychiatry in March 1955, Calvin College, Grand Rapids, Mich. The conference dealt with the topic "The Place of the Christian Conception of Sin in the Theory and Practice of Psychiatry."

Adam and Eve knew their nakedness, their guilt. They heard God and fled in fear. They feared the consequences of their act and offered excuses. In effect this was a refusal to accept reality. People have refused to accept their true creature–Creator relationship ever since, expressing their rebellion by formulating every conceivable substitute for God. They flee religiopsychological mechanisms that are fatal without God but life-generating if they would only allow God's miraculous intervention to drive them to him.

Through what we call psychosomatics, the same psychological processes have altered and degenerated our physical resistance to forces over which we once had perfect control. In our effort to demonstrate omniscience and omnipotence, we have disrupted nature so that it is at enmity with us. We have available to us other religiopsychological mechanisms and experiences, such as comfort, belongingness, confession, atonement, sacrifice, forgiveness, acceptance, approval, and a sense of adequacy. In relation with Jehovah-God, these experiences produce a true sonship to the Father, atonement through Christ, and the guidance of the Holy Spirit.

Nevertheless, men and women have blindly, desperately worshiped anything—sticks and stones, rivers and frogs, Molechs and Baals. More noticeable today are their attempts to escape the external need for salvation. Confronted by the Christ of the incarnation, they stumble over and miss his essential meaning. They believe that the answer is within themselves and that they can establish themselves before God. They have refused Christ through pride, rationalization, neutrality, or neglect, and have assumed a sort of Jehovah–Messiah complex—"I'll save myself in my own way." This original sin, and its effects on culture, reason, theory, and other human endeavors, are still with us and have conditioned us even in our approach to the subject at hand.

I believe that humankind, in its attempt to find comfort, has set up what I shall call Baals as god-surrogates. These Baals may be blatantly immoral, or they may appear to be good from a horizontally determined, person-formulated code of ethics and values. The religiopsychological mechanisms work within persons when they attempt to satisfy these Baals, whether good or bad, producing the discomfort of guilt. There is something of the principle of the Abrahamic covenant or the Joshua compact here. That is to say, even as parents have chosen a set of Baals, so also their children are conditioned to such worship or aspiration. This conditioning is found in tradition, church, school, home, society, the arts, government, everywhere.

To the extent that persons can squelch what remnant of God-desire is in them and feel satisfied with the degree to which they have answered to these Baals, to that degree they should feel comfortable. But persons cannot rest in a substitute god, as Augustine reminds us when he says, "Our hearts were made for Thee; they are restless until they rest in Thee, O God." The result is that there is an almost universal neurosis. Persons seek hope in mirages. They refuse, unless changed by the grace of God, to seek out or to find the eternal vision, and with these substrata of universal neurosis, they find it difficult to face the inescapable discomforts of life.

Even those who have sought the true God find it difficult to differentiate Jehovah-God from good Baals. Or, having made the differentiation, they suffer the effects of six thousand years of Baal conditioning. In such individuals one may well attempt to develop the concept of glorious suffering, that is, the paradoxical realization that a measure of discomfort is a great source of comfort. A truly christocentric individual cannot be content to live horizontally. Contentment lies in the vertical plane. There is a patient but urgent seeking after what Augustine calls the "city of God." This is a contentment which rests in the eternal hope.

From a clinical standpoint, the Jehovah–Messiah self-delusion provokes a fist-shaking, God-cursing rebellion. It permits, with an omnipotent spirit, complete irresponsibility, a fantastic reality denial, a self-created delusion. It may even produce the paradox of self-withdrawal for the purpose of self-preservation, a spore-like life in a sort of omnipotent abandon. In other attempts to escape reality, there is a quantitative, if not a qualitative, denial of the facts through expansiveness and exultation, or through complete self-effacement and even self-annihilation. In less obvious escapes, there are the somatic outlets and somatic accompaniments of tension. The relation of failure or sin to emotional displacement, transfer, identification, and compensation need not be detailed here.

What of the attempt to alter the body's physical and chemical processes in an effort to produce comfort, or to alter the sensitivity or reactivity of the individual with sedation, electrical manipulation, or even surgery? I believe nothing should be done that will permanently alter patients' ability to evaluate themselves and their creature–Creator relationship. As psychiatrists, we may bring patients to a proper appreciation of the existence of Baals in their lives. As Christian psychiatrists, we must help patients to differentiate between the so-called good Baals and Jehovah-God. We must strive to point out the need for dethroning Baal with all of his cohorts and to humbly enthrone Jehovah-God with his saving grace. We must attempt to free patients from the prostitution of their religiopsychological mechanisms and direct them to use their forces for their eternal welfare.

When Scripture speaks of life, we are tempted to say, "figure of speech," "not applicable," "oversimplification," forgetting that persons are spiritual beings with psychophysical means of expression. We are apt to forget that a person's only reason for being is to know God and to love him with the whole personality and that all of our psychological and physical-chemical processes were meant originally for that purpose. In all of human life, there is one true ambivalence—whether God's will be done or mine. God's will is fundamental to all living, a principle to which all of our psychological and somatic functioning must become subservient if there is to be comfort. This subservience means God-centered authority, christocentric thinking, and Spirit-motivated living, a faith-inspired sense of belonging and adequacy. It means God-like love in contrast with indulgent permissiveness or possessiveness motivated by frustration. It means authority, which is an expression of God, rather than reactive self-assertiveness or pseudoomniscience and pseudoomnipotence. It means love of God in contrast with envy, avarice, jealousy, and all of the other interpersonal vices. It means God-provoked vengeance in contrast with ego-centered grudges, hates, and vindictiveness. It means soul work in contrast with material possessions or social acceptance. It means a philosophy of life which will evoke the sacrifice of anything and everything for Christ.

This philosophy must be fundamental to our intrapersonal and interpersonal life. Anything less is sin. Commitment to Christ must become so much a part of what we do and what we think or say that all Baals will be dethroned and all alliances with Baal will cease. Then we will restore the religiopsychological mechanisms to their legitimate task of redirecting human beings to their Creator. Then pain—even the psychological pain of imperfection—will be almost lost in the fundamental contentment which is rooted in him in whom we have believed, in him who is able to keep that which we have committed to him against the last day.

Sin and Sickness—An Uneasy Dialogue:
Ralph Heynen

Traditionally, there has been a conflict between psychologists and theologians in Reformed circles. There is even a bit of suspicion between them, although whether the suspicion indicates an insecurity on the part of theologians or among the psychologists is difficult to determine.

It is well to remember that psychology and theology are different disciplines: the one falls in the field of natural science and the other in the field of spiritual science. Calvinism, however, stresses the unity among the sciences; we are not to separate life into little compartments but must try to embrace them within one life view. While noting that inclusivity, I believe that each discipline is to uphold the sovereignty of its own field. The psychologist is not entitled to speak with supreme authority in the field of theology nor is the theologian to speak with supreme authority in the field of psychology. Nevertheless, we should develop a greater understanding of and need for each other in both theory and practice.

In terms of sin and guilt, we are moving in the terrain of both the theologian and the psychologist. Anyone who deals intimately with the lives of people cannot escape the fact that sin is a vital part of the warp and woof of humanity. Since I believe that this is especially evident in people who are mentally and emotionally ill I am surprised that there are only a few books on the subject. Most books on classical psychology do not even mention the term *sin;* they may speak about guilt but the concept of sin is largely ignored. Nevertheless, I think there is a definite relation between sin and mental illness. If there were no sin there would be no sickness, including no mental illness. I am not saying that sin causes sickness, but that all people become sick with some illness because they are sinners.

The question becomes: "What is the relationship between sin and sickness?" I think three relationships are clearly indicated in the Bible. The first is that sickness is a matter of punishment for sin, as was true in the case of the wicked men in the days of Noah. A just God punishes people for what they have done or have not done. The second relationship is that of chastisement. An illustration of chastisement is found in the case of Manasseh. Chastisement is always related to a specific sin, and it is always sent in the spirit of love to save sinners or to lead them to a fuller life. A third way to relate sin and suffering is through the idea of testing, as, for example, in the case of Abraham when he is asked to sacrifice his son or in the case of Job when his faith is being tested. There is no mention of a specific sin in these cases. Instead God is putting his children through the crucible to remove the dross and to encourage genuine faith and noble character.

It may be hard for us to say in any particular situation which of the three relationships is applicable. If it is the first or second, there is a direct connection between sin and sickness. If it is a matter of testing, as I believe it often is for a child of God, then it is difficult to determine if there is any interrelationship between the individual's sickness and sin. Thus it is difficult to lay down absolute principles or to speak in a dogmatic way. To a large extent each case must be judged on an individual basis.

In practice it is often difficult to determine whether an erratic behavior is sin or symptom. Whereas sin is unbelief, a turning from God, a symptom indicates the disintegration of a personality or a diseased personality. In general, when we deal with psychotic patients, it is not difficult to determine that the actions and the words, the behavior and the gestures, are symptoms rather than sins. The question becomes more complex, however, when we are dealing with neurotic or borderline psychotic cases. Here it is good to move with caution.

The tendency to explain all evil behavior on the basis of symptoms, and never on the basis of sin, can be dangerous and morally fatal to future generations. It leads to the diminution of personal responsibility. There is something within the human personality that enables us to rise above heredity or the environment. Thus, trying to account for all human actions on the basis of determinism alone can be morally harmful. At the other extreme are those who say that sin is sin and must be treated as such. They deny that the troubled person is driven by forces beyond his or her control. They insist that such persons are sinners and that they must be held personally accountable. Much harm has been done by this approach, for it fails to take seriously the reality of sickness over against the power of sin.

We stand before two realities. On the one hand we must not ignore the effect of disease on human behavior. On the other hand we must witness to the renewed conviction that the reality of sin cannot be ignored. The whole matter may come down to a question of responsibility. Is the person responsible for a particular action or not? Is the action to be regarded as sin or as symptom? There are no clear guidelines. Each situation must be judged on its own in light of the person's total personality and all the motivating factors that operate within that personality. At the same time, we must not negate personal responsibility and replace the concept of sin with the concept of disease. Instead the two concepts must be carefully applied to the situation to see which is relevant. The ultimate decision, of course, rests in the hands of God, the One who is far wiser and far more loving than we are. Above all we should avoid the pretension that we have final answers when in fact we do not.

4

Sin and Sickness: The Nature of Human Failure

J. HAROLD ELLENS

Western society, religious and secular alike, relies to a large extent upon some concept of sin to undergird its value system. Religious persons generally base their systems of right and wrong, appropriateness, and legitimate esteem upon the notion that there are behaviors which are sinful because they break relationships and breach codes of correctness or acceptability. The judgment as to what is sin or sinful is based upon a perception of what God expects or requires. Conforming to God's requirements or fulfilling his expectations deserves moral approbation. It is a fulfillment of our God-given nature and destiny. Failing to meet those expectations is a denial of, and a failure to actualize, our true nature and destiny. Such failure is moral turpitude and deserves moral judgment.

The secular society participates much more extensively in this mindset than it usually acknowledges. Perhaps this is the remnant of Judeo-Christian ethics which have permeated Western culture or it may be that the sin-concept, upon which both religious and secular society depend for their value structures, derives from some primordial source in the human psyche. In any case, even secular society operates with the notion that there are general categories of behavior which conform to accepted standards of function and relationship and are approvable for that reason, and there are others which do not measure up and are, therefore, punishable as immoral. They are sin.

When Karl Menninger wrote *Whatever Became of Sin?*, he intended to call America back to morality and to responsible relationship between people and their environment. As a well-known psychiatrist he surprised and pleased the general public by voicing a shared concern about the erosion of moral responsibility. He also spoke for many of us when he implied that the success of sociology and psychology as a molding force had resulted in the deterioration of order and responsibility in our society. He seemed to endorse our need to have law, sin, punishment, and salvation clearly identified and responsibly considered.

Menninger defined sin as rebellion and alienation, acted out in aggressive ways that hurt others or that despoil the created world. He saw it as a failure to give and receive love. His illustrations were mainly related to ecological irresponsibility, insensitivity to the needy, and national policies that waste America's natural and human resources. His book claimed that much of what has been passed off as psychological distortion or social dysfunction is willful moral aberration—a breaking of the law and a violation of our true nature and destiny. He claimed that sin is disobedience and hence a moral issue and that it is alienation from our true selves and from each other and hence a matter of broken relationship and violation of the covenant we have with each other and our world.

Menninger was attempting to correct an imbalance. He felt that misbehavior had been so socialized and psychologized that humans felt exempt from taking responsibility for their behavior. He maintained that the deterioration of order and idealism was the result of the psychological rationalization of moral evil which undercut personal accountability and discipline. He urged us to return to the notion of sin as the real nature of our irresponsibility and to reinstate guilt as an effective motivator of appropriate behavior.

At this point, Menninger makes a fatal shift in emphasis. He absorbs into his notion of sin as moral transgression his more basic concept that sin is alienation of the self from its true destiny, that is, from that set of relationships in which it is designed to find its fulfillment and meaning. Such relationships are with God, self, others, and the material world. So sin as breaking relationship is equated with the more trivial matter of sin as breaking the law or moral code. As a result, Menninger falls into an erroneous perspective typical of the secular American world and of the conservative Christian world. He reduces sin to moral failure and defines moral failure as transgression of codes or regulations.

According to Menninger when a person's behavior does not conform to the moral order, that person is blamable and should feel guilty. Appropriate guilt will motivate the person to change and to behave in a correct manner. So moral standards produce a sense of immorality in persons who fall short of them. This awareness engenders a proper sense of sin and will induce feelings of guilt. Guilt, in turn, will motivate good behavior which will, in turn, reinforce the moral order. Menninger's formula expresses our desire to hold on to the concept of sin for its utilitarian value—praise and blame are used to motivate us to face our moral dilemma. We have here a sin-guilt-judgment-justice-justification-sanctification model of the human predicament.

Menninger's scheme sounds good, even biblical, since the Bible uses the concept of sin to describe the human predicament. Nevertheless we are led to ask: Is sin the best term to describe what ails us, or given our understanding of human dynamics, would "sickness" work as well or even better?

It seems clear that the term we use to describe the nature of human failure must express at least three things. It must describe the brokenness of the relationships essential to our achievement of our true destiny. It must describe our proclivity to break the rules of moral responsibility. It must describe the systemic disorder which prevents us from lifting ourselves out of our forlorn predicament. Moreover, the term must imply an appropriate theology of salvation. It should include the biblical concepts of reconciliation of broken relationships, the forgiveness of transgressions and of our proclivity to commit them, and the healing of the systemic disorder that prevents us from either avoiding our tragedy or healing it ourselves. It is not self-evident whether *sin* or *sickness* is the more adequate concept for the task. What is self-evident is our tendency to limit the notions of sin and salvation to the sin-guilt-judgment-justice-justification-sanctification model. This tendency can reduce the concept of sin to only a juridical matter.

Overemphasizing a juridical concept of sin implies that the human problem is wholly moral culpability and God's primary response is a praise-blame disposition toward us. Human disorder is treated only by the regimens of punishment or the strategies of self-expiatory forgiveness. Used in this way, the concept of sin seems to convey quite a different and more limited notion than what the Bible intends.

Just as it is unbiblical to pour different content into the term *sin* than what it was intended to carry, so it would be unbiblical to import from the Bible a culture-bound term which in our century fails to describe adequately the predicament the Bible intends to address. This is particularly true of concepts that describe our humanness, since these often do not communicate with our sociological and psychological understanding of human personhood. We are morally and exegetically bound to employ for our culture terms that accurately express the notion of human failure and its remedy, thereby preserving the biblical intent and the contemporary understanding.

Specifically we ask: When we talk about the human predicament, are we talking about sin or sickness? Which concept more adequately describes the human condition as we know it today?

Setting the Course

Numerous issues are implied in our questions. Some of the more important ones are: What does the Bible say about human disorder and what is crucial in its intent? What has the church historically intended to address in its use of the term *sin*, and did it have the real issues accurately in mind? Does Menninger's scheme for moral renewal really work or is there a better alternative? What is the dynamic relationship between sin and grace and God's goal for constructive development in human beings? Is the basic problem that obstructs ideal human function perversity or illness, that is, is evil in humans moral disorder, alienation from our own true nature, or pathology? If moral disorder, does the term inevitably place this disorder under the heading of sin, or can it more accurately refer to failure resulting from ignorance, psychological distortions, or sociological deprivations? Is human personality renovated by the threat of law or by the structures inherent in love? What is the nature of guilt and how effectively does it function in human renovation?

The Bible and Sin

Scripture has no word that is exactly equivalent to the English word *sin*. A large variety of Greek and Hebrew words are employed to describe various aspects of disorder in our relationship with God. All the words intend to call our attention to relational dysfunction or inappropriateness of some kind. Behind these biblical terms and concepts lies the root idea that in creation and in covenant God deals with us with the ideal that relationship to him is our proper destiny. That relationship implies that as people stand in covenant with God they also stand in covenant with themselves, with each other, and with the universe as well. Their task is to act in such a way that the whole community of humanity and the entire cosmos might achieve divinely intended self-actualization and manifest the glorious imagination of our creative God. This is true fulfillment.

All other alternatives that we pursue express and reinforce our alienating narcissism. Preoccupation with such alternatives is, according to Scripture, symptomatic of our universal and perpetual predicament. The endogenous and endemic quality of that disorder is what the Bible refers to in all the Greek and Hebrew words we subsume under the English conception of sin.

In the Old Testament the words are:

1. *ḥattā't*, a failure to achieve exactly what was expected—"a missing"
2. *pesa'*, a failure to conform to the standard—"a rebellion"
3. *peša'*, a failure to do things just the way they were required—"a transgression"
4. *'awon*, a distortion or corruption of that for which one was intended—"a perversion"
5. *ra'*, a nastiness of disposition—"evil"

6. *reša'*, an insensitivity to that which would be appropriate to a child of God living before the face of God—"impiety."

The New Testament words for sin have a similar character and content. They include:

1. *hamartia,* a failure to achieve exactly what was expected—"missing the mark"
2. *parabasis,* a failure to do things just the way they were required—"a transgression"
3. *adikia,* a failure to conform to the standard and thus a falling into behavior which is not affirmed or approved—"unrighteousness"
4. *asebeia,* an insensitivity to that which would be appropriate to a child of God living before the face of God—"impiety"
5. *anomia,* a failure to adhere to prescriptions—"lawlessness"
6. *ponēria,* an inability to do right and good—"depravity"
7. *epithymia,* a longing to do differently from what is appropriate and prescribed—"evil desire."

The relational orientation of all these terms has three aspects. They refer to our failure to do, to achieve, or to reflect God's ideal design for us. They refer derivatively to the way in which our relationship with others is affected by our failure to express God's ideal design and expectation. They convey the idea of a fracture and distortion of God's image in our natures, the *imago Dei.* The notion of fulfilling God's design and expectation is intended in Scripture to express the dynamic possibilities of our life and growth as children of God who are made in his image. It can easily be reduced, however, to a mere measuring up to God's legal standards, thus reducing the grand theological notion to a moral formula.

Already in Scripture and throughout the history of the church, there has been a strong tendency toward just such a reducing of the human condition to a superficial, legalistic misapplication of the justice-justification continuum. Such reductionism sees issues in terms of praise and blame, and every aberration becomes a moral issue and not an issue of human limitation, inadequacy, ignorance, or illness.

In this model it is not an ontological reality that forces the praise-blame formula, but the human conceptual model that happens to be in vogue at the time. Praise and blame are the most primitive and prevalent categories in human history for managing the shadow side of our humanness. They are simple to use in responding to what is uncomfortable, unacceptable, or unexpected. If justification is taken out of this primitive legalistic formula, however, justice can take its proper place as the ground for justification in a model of radical grace—what Martin Luther saw so clearly and redemptively when he spoke of the *righteousness* in God in which he forgives us when it seems unjust, unfair, and immoral to do so.

Scripture speaks of praise and blame, but the distinctive word of the gospel, unique to Judaism and Christianity, is not praise and blame but grace. The word arises not from a juridical justice-justification model but out of unconditional mercy and tough love. It is a formula for freedom within structure, unconditional affirmation with guidance, unconditional acceptance for the purpose of stimulating growth and godly self-actualization. God did not react negatively to our shadow side but in grace relates with incredible positive regard for us despite our distortion and awfulness, indeed because of our hopeless condition. God is in the business of healing, not of condemning, as John 3:17 makes clear, "God did not send his Son into the world to condemn the world, but to save the world through him" (NIV).

A juridical, law-oriented use of the justice-justification model is far too optimistic. It fails to consider the fact that we are not capable of becoming just and right. We need grace, God's unconditional embrace, with freedom to grow in his grace. This removes all hope from strategies in which we try to become "right with God" and places all hope in God alone.

The biblical message of grace and discipline has extraordinary import for us, because it stands in contrast to any legalistic and superficial message of justice and justification. It is especially important, because of the way it relates grace and tough love in light of the biblical notion of our real nature. The Bible portrays humanity as moving along a continuum from the naive and primitive condition of an idyllic garden paradise through rebellion and disengagement. It shows humanity's failure to return to God through external authority (law) but human success to mature through responsible kingdom building and adherence to the discipline of the internal authority of full-orbed personhood in Christ.

The pattern is one of growth and maturation toward God's ultimate intention for us. It is a process that is intensely individual and existential, though it takes place in a significant communal context and reflects deep, undergirding principles of developmental structure and providence. It is a growth process in which we are afforded total freedom to think, feel, and behave as we wish without fear that we shall fall out of God's grace. At the same time it is a process in which behavior has consequences and maturing means taking responsibility for those consequences.

Taking responsibility is painful. Our behavior always moves out of ignorance, human limitation, narcissistic needs, and inadequate imagination. This generates anxiety and rebellion that make our disorder so aggressive and revolutionary, so willful and alienating. Moreover, when we endeavor to take responsibility we discover that it always operates in a world of divine opportunity, unimaginable possibilities, and eternal significance. We are invited to God-sized tasks but have only human resources. We are called to love one another, but our human limitations, our generic anxiety, and our own narcissistic neediness make us inherently incapable of doing that well. We feel inadequate to the responsibilities of life and the challenges of godliness because we are, in fact, inadequate. It is inevitable that we feel guilty, because we fall short in our own judgment and in reality as we measure ourselves in terms of God's ideal for us. This dilemma is stated poignantly in Romans 3:23, and Paul's answer follows immediately.

The answer is that the gospel of God's grace is tailored precisely to this situation in that it is unconditional, radical, and universally available. It is designed to deliver us from both useless feelings of guilt and from real acts of distortion and failure. We are delivered by his declaration that none of these things (our guilt, distortion, failure, and evil) need to count with him. They all can be washed away. So the Word of God can say with utter seriousness that Christ was exalted so that "every knee should bow, in heaven and on earth and under the earth, and every tongue should confess that Jesus Christ is Lord, to the glory of God the Father" (Phil. 2:10–11 NIV).

Nevertheless, behavior has consequences in life. If a person walks off the roof of a house, he or she will suffer the consequences. It is true to the structure of the universe that the law of gravity operates. Or if one abuses a spouse for thirty years, one is liable to die a lonely person. It is true to the structure of God's universe that the psychological and social laws of cause and effect also hold up. Finally, if a person ignores the God question all of life, or distorts it, that person will end up in a place of unresolvable spiritual loneliness and confusion. The laws of spiritual reality hold as surely as do the laws of physics and psychology.

We live with the consequences of our inadequacies and distortions. We must hold ourselves and each other accountable, even when we cannot find the resources to be accountable. We grow from pain and from the divine and human love we experience in the middle of pain. Only by holding ourselves accountable for the consequences of our behavior in spite of our ultimate inability to be accountable, will we generate the requisite kind of pain for growth. Biblically, we are talking about unconditional grace and tough love: Grace is the context and matrix in which we function; discipline is the structure which provokes growth in that context. It is indeed a special act of divine grace that behavior has consequences and that by the tough love of accountability we grow toward God's ideal for us. We mature.

Scripture recognizes clearly that we tend to avoid the consequences of our behavior by passing them along to others. There are many caring or neurotic people who are willing to absorb the pain of our behavior and its consequences, often to their own detriment. However genuine or positive in intent, they frequently do not do us a favor. Their graciousness deprives us of the pain that would move us to necessary growth and maturation. Tough love in the matrix of divine grace provides stimulus for psychological and spiritual growth without the trappings of the legalistic form of the justice-justification formula. It does its redemptive work to remove the need for judgment and condemnation.

Overwhelming pain, of course, destroys. God offers rescue from that ultimate possibility by his grace, and we are called to modulate each other's pain to the extent that that aids growth. Pastoring is about that and so is Christian love. Nevertheless, holding out for appropriate Christian discipline, which provides structure for growth even if it is painful, is also an act of love and grace. It avoids the temptation to rescue and instead forces one to cope and thereby to grow. Christian discipline is not an expression of the legalistic or juridical justice-justification model. It is radical grace in its most practical applied expression. Its motive and objective are to enhance and stimulate growth, not to shape people up.

Historical Considerations

Throughout its history the church has tended to cast the issue of human failure in a legalistic justice-justification construct. In general, the result is a formulation of human error and estrangement in terms of an adversarial relationship between God and the human race. If this does not reflect the distinctive contribution of the Judeo-Christian gospel it is more typical of non-Judeo-Christian religions.

This superficial form of the justice-justification formula has often prevailed in Western Christendom. The formula is universal in human religious philosophies. It appears in the shaman's enterprise of god-control by fetish and incantation. It is visible in some American Christians' pursuit of self-justification through obsessive conformity to rigid codes of conduct, ecclesiastical prescription, or theological propositions, and in the liturgist's adherence to sacred rituals to satisfy God. The issue is the same—human attempts to balance God's requirements for rectitude and justification.

The same process goes on in the soul of the healthy person who worries inappropriately about whether or not he or she is pleasing to God. It also goes on in the soul of the psychologically ill person who obsesses about guilt, shame, or ritual needs for purification and self-justification. Behind it all is the apparently inherent human proclivity to feel unworthy or inadequate and to try to achieve anxiety reduction and increased security with God by *doing* something right.

This need to control our environment and God seems to be born out of this universal sense of inadequacy and unworthiness. At birth we are expelled from the secure world of the womb into a radically alien world. We are fragile, dependent, and wholly vulnerable. We spend a lifetime attempting to increase our control of the environment, hoping thereby to reduce our anxiety. We succeed to some degree but fall short of achieving satisfactory security in many ways. We reduce our anxiety and resolve our sense of inadequacy on some fronts but experience limitations and a sense of unworthiness throughout life. We interpret our situation to mean that we are undesirable, under judgment, and not measuring up to God's expectations. Our response is to believe that we must control God to protect ourselves from his judgment, to placate him with things that please him, and to work to justify ourselves before his face. We get caught in a superficial and legalistic justice-justification formula that is psychologically and spiritually primitive and non-Christian.

God's message is distinctively different. It is good news about grace, cutting the tap root of the legalistic formula, by declaring that God is for us, not against us. It maintains that the destructive, adversarial idea of God is answered by the gospel. Where the non-Christian formula prevails, the tap root of the gospel of grace is destroyed.

Psychospiritual Dynamics

In the grace-discipline model of expressing the gospel, the issue of free will and the legitimacy of our choices arises. In a sense we all have free will, so that we can be held accountable to structured and informed discipline and, as a consequence, grow from the pain that such accountability and discipline prompts. Our free will, however, is only a proximate kind. It is bound by our nature, not just by our sinful nature but also by our created nature. We can will only that to which our hearts hold allegiance. In other words, we are bound psychologically and spiritually by the prevailing value system, love objects, and principles of allegiance to which our lives are given at any moment. These determinants are largely unconscious and characterological, remaining subvolitional and sub-rational. They tend to be culture- and time-bound.

We are bound by a kind of addictive allegiance to that to which our hearts are wedded. It may be to self; it can be to Christ. Being driven by generic anxiety from birth on, we are addicted to ourselves and to the consequent psychological and spiritual distortion. We can be healed and delivered only by God's unconditional grace. This grace declares that our distortion and perversity need not count in any transcendent or ultimate sense. God's grace is all that counts. It relieves us of the need to be and do the ideal and frees us to grow and to accept our own limited and sick human nature.

We do evil when we follow our narcissistic selves and inflict injury or disadvantage upon fellow human beings or upon God's world. The evil results from bad choices that are free in the proximate sense but bound in the ultimate sense of unconscious commitment to unhealthful values. It comes from ignorance, psychopathology, spiritual pathology, inadequacy, and other human limitations and distortions. Where there is proximate freedom of the will, bad choices can and will be made. That fact certifies the reality of freedom in a world in which humans are ultimately limited and cannot foresee all or control all, not even in their own souls and psyches.

This is a good and lovely world in spite of the painful consequences of human distortion and bad choices. It is a world in which, despite our ultimate bondage, we are free to will and to choose in terms of the underlying commitment of our hearts, whether we are committed by faith or by psychopathology. We can see the consequences of our choices and to a limited and proximate degree take them seriously, modify them, and grow from them. However, we can be delivered from the hopelessness of our ultimate bondage only by God's declaration that it does not count against us, his affirmation of us.

As we have seen, sin is our failure to keep covenantal relationships which are, in fact, our true fulfillment as people of God. Our failure includes falling short of the expectations that God and others have for our covenant relationships. We fail to be who we are, made in God's likeness and called to be his colaborers in building his reign of love and grace in the lives and institutions of humankind.

The Bible's numerous terms for our failure indicate that humankind cannot deliver itself from its plight or rise above the inclination to fail. Only special intervention from God can effect deliverance and change. Any strategy for self-justification is inherently blasphemous and runs counter to the central and essential nature of the gospel. Works righteousness and the gospel of grace stand in sharp contrast to each other.

The Bible, then, describes a condition that is irremedial except by divine intervention. Sin is alienation, a moral failure in a setting in which the alternative is the possibility of living up to God's ideal for us. The ideal is implied in our very nature and is articulated by God in his laws and counsels. It is impossible to achieve, because humankind has neither the understanding, imagination, vision, volition, or orientation adequate to such an achievement. Humans are flawed, and the flaw is so deep, so critical in character, so systemic, that no one escapes the infection, disorder, or distortion. We are not as bad as we can possibly be, but according to the Bible we are never able to achieve the best that God intended. We miss the mark and are dead or helpless in this condition of trespass and rebellion.

The Bible indicates that our condition is infinitely worse than the English word *sin* has come to imply in popular usage. Our condition is far worse than mere moral turpitude. It is lack of faith and lostness. To suggest that our problem is merely a legalistic fault that can be cancelled by our juridical acts of balancing the scales of justice, is to see the human predicament far too optimistically. Humans are enslaved and are redeemable only by grace. Sin, if understood in a superficial way, is an inadequate metaphor for describing the human condition. The main thrust in Scripture from Genesis to the Apocalypse asserts that humans are sick unto death and cannot survive without healing. It is because we are not merely transgressors but profoundly alienated and lost that the messianic Savior comes to us "with healing in his wings."

The Church and Sin

Historically, the church has emphasized that sin is human dysfunction which causes a failure in the covenant relationship in which God cherishes us and sustains us in life and fellowship with himself. Disobeying the will and expectations of God has always been an aspect of sin. Frequently, as indicated above, the matter of disobedience has been expressed in terms of human lack of conformity to God's expressed ideals for humankind. Generally speaking, the church has included in this emphasis notions of objective disobedience to specific laws and of subjective failures in relationality. In more heroic moments, it has seen clearly and proclaimed accurately the biblical perspective on sin and grace. The tragedy, however, is that the church has tended in every age to slide toward legalism in issues related to ethics, morality, and covenant commitments. As a corollary, it has tended to proclaim or imply a conditional grace based in part on outwardly proper behavior.

The unique religious breakthrough in history was Abraham's faith in God as a God who arbitrarily covenants with a people and unconditionally embraces them in his forgiving and redeeming grace. This revelation shaped the essential contours of Judaism and Christianity, distinguishing them in an absolute sense from all other religions. Judaism eventually reduced its transcendent covenantal vision into legalistic works righteousness, boiling down Israel's commitment to formal prescriptions of liturgical and social law. Thus conformity was affirmed and rewarded while disobedience to the codes and prescriptions was punished. This terrestrial order was justified by and telescoped into divine order. The human problem was seen as one of only outward transgressions which required payment or repair. Human lostness was reduced to mere legalistic sinfulness and God's grace to conditional approval, dependent upon behavior and achievement.

Jesus cut through legalistic Judaism and made finally sure the covenant of unconditional grace, indelibly writing it upon the pages of Scripture and history with his blood-stained cross of Calvary. But in two centuries the mainstream of Christianity introduced into this new believing community the model of Hellenistic Judaism. Christian thought regarding sin and grace deteriorated into the legalism of medieval theology. The human predicament was seen as transgression of finite laws which was remedied by righteous compensations either by oneself or by others on one's behalf.

This view of sin implied a formal, nearly materialistic, view of grace that was wholly conditional. The integrating concept or framework for these notions was a juridical model. It was, in effect, an optimistic Christian humanism that assumed that world order was structured by divine and human law, that the problem was human disobedience, that the consequence was guilt and condemnation, and that the solution was payment by self, Christ, or the saints. Grace became the gift of that solution on the condition of petition or payment and for the tenure of obedience. The process followed a logical sequence: A law was transgressed; a judgment made; a sentence pronounced; a payment effected; justice was served, and the culprit was justified.

This erroneous system failed to comprehend the covenant nature of our life with God, the relational character and alienation of sin, the loss of our true selves and our authentic destiny, and the unconditional reality of grace as God's arbitrary act to restore the covenant. It failed to realize that appropriated grace is the divine restoration of ourselves to our true natures in spite of ourselves.

The Protestant Reformation was driven by an increasing awareness of the gross inadequacy of the legalistic model. John Huss, John Wycliff, Desiderius Erasmus, Martin Luther, Jean Calvin, Philip Melanchthon, and others saw that the concept was biblically inaccurate and theologically unsound. In today's terminology they might have added that the model was culturally time-bound and psychologically or spiritually dysfunctional. Luther saw that it was too optimistic regarding the human predicament of disorder and too pessimistic regarding the true character of God's intervention on our behalf. The Reformers realized that the good news of the gospel had been lost. Unfortunately, Protestant scholasticism and other forces eclipsed this clear vision in less than two hundred years.

Historically, then, the church has been dominated primarily by a superficial view of the human problem and of God's solution. For this reason it has been enamored by the metaphor of sin, understood in a legalistic and superficial way, and consequently it has deprived itself of a genuinely biblical understanding of the human predicament. It does not appreciate our total inability to make ourselves right with God, to heal our relationship with him. As a corollary, the church has tended to be satisfied with a superficial notion of salvation, failing to appreciate how we are caught in a trap of immorality or irresponsibility from which we cannot extricate ourselves. Our problem is not merely that we are not good at relationships or that we are breakers of the law. Our problem is that we are so flawed, so ignorant, so inadequate to the responsibilities of life and the challenges of godliness, that we are inherently covenant breakers and relationship defilers. There is no health in us.

It is my conviction that more of what the Bible says about our spiritual sickness needs to be introduced into our understanding of sin, if we are to restore the authentic biblical teaching and to give grace its necessary place at the heart of the gospel. The biblical concept of sin is multidimensional and its deeper meaning is enhanced by the biblical understanding of our psychospiritual sickness.

God's Grace and the Human Condition

The problem that the believing community has had with the biblical concept of grace is that the idea is so radical in both the Hebrew Bible and the New Testament. God's grace is represented as an arbitrary intervention on behalf of humankind. It is announced and not negotiated, covenanted by God from his side and guaranteed. It is effective for us in spite of ourselves. Furthermore, it does not merely treat our symptoms of disobedience, ignorance, or unbelief but moves past those symptoms to our sickness. That root sickness is a deficit and disorder in our very nature whereby we are alienated from God without consciously choosing to be, without comprehending the full tragic import of it, and without any ability to remedy it. It is a sickness in that it is a condition of our nature, not merely a malfunction of our intent or behavior. Moreover, it is a sickness in that it infects every aspect of our personhood and all facets of the cosmos. It is a disease in us that leaves everything about us fractured, limited, and infectious. We are not simply plagued by a tendency to do evil. We are evil. And we infect each other, our children, our community, and our world with an infection that becomes a disposition of our hearts, an orientation of our intellects, a pattern of our emotions, and a response of our spirits. The infection pervades our entire organism, individual and communal.

The sin that is sickness gives rise to all manner of psychological and spiritual reaction formation, defensiveness, and secondary distortions and symptomology. This development complicates our situation, making it difficult for us to see the real problem from which we suffer. It is a fulminating infection until the grace of God enters into our psychospiritual process and reduces the infection.

The radical character of the gospel is that it declares the irremedial disorder erased. It declares that our sickness and our anxiety or guilt about it may be healed by grace alone. But radical grace is undesirable to us for two reasons: First, it requires that we abandon ourselves to God without any hope of improving our leverage with him. We are not to be vindicated but simply to be declared acceptable. Second, we can no longer live by the power of conditional strategies for relating to or controlling our relationships with other people and with God's creation. The issue of life becomes healing and growth, not power and justice. That is God's special kind of redemption, specifically prepared for just such a predicament as ours.

Unconditional grace relates ingeniously to the facts that we know about the human condition. From theology, psychology, and sociology we know that a large variety of factors play significant roles in human attitude, function, and behavior. Biochemistry, genetics, prenatal environment, childhood conditions, inadvertent loss of love objects, processes of puberty, adolescent conditions, environment, peers, and spiritual training are a few of the factors that play concrete and identifiable roles in our formation.

In the debate about nature versus nurture it is increasingly clear that a great deal more is nature than was supposed fifty years ago in the days of John Dewey. Shortly, I think, we will have in hand data to confirm that 70 percent of everything in human formation is genetic and biochemical and only 30 percent is environmental. Indeed, those figures may be extremely conservative. In any case, it is clear that people do not choose the shape of their development physically, psychologically, or spiritually. They are not able to influence their internal development significantly, except in terms of the content they choose to pour into their physiology by their appetites, into their psychology by the acquaintances or pursuits they choose, and into their spirits by the way they worship or celebrate God. That content is a limited proportion of their total developmental dynamics.

The shape of human behavior, then, is under our control in only a proximate, and not an ultimate, sense. We can choose between chocolate and vanilla, work and play, medicine and law, blondes and brunettes, and the like, but these are relatively superficial levels of choice. And even they may be driven by unconscious predilections to a far greater degree than we wish to acknowledge.

Given the degree to which our thoughts and actions are determined, any notion of sin that assumes that we freely choose to do good or ill and that we are, in that sense, fully responsible for doing so and for changing the course of behavior or for correcting evil, is a notion that needs to be seriously reconsidered, lest we be guilty of a kind of abuse of suffering humankind.

The reconsideration ought to pour more biblical content into our theology of sin by emphasizing our inherent sickness, psychologically and spiritually. The Bible acknowledges the desperate nature of our sickness but is wholly preoccupied with our prospects for healing and the subsequent restoration of the wholeness of the entire creation. Biblical theology represents the human condition in ways that are infinitely hopeless in human terms and infinitely hopeful in divine terms. The human problem is our inherent disorder, our sickness, our disease. We are orphans cut off from God and incapable of repairing that condition and the misbehaviors that come from it. When we shift our inquiry from the question of how we got into such a bad state to the question of what can be done about it, the sickness and health metaphor brings a great deal of helpful new insight to the meaning of God's passion for us and his redemptive strategies on our behalf. The prospect for us is that we can now and forever be cherished as we are, in spite of ourselves, growing from the pain of our ambiguity into the full potential personhood of those who are in Christ Jesus. We are sick unto death, but we shall be healed. John says:

> I saw a new heaven and a new earth . . . I saw the Holy City, the new Jerusalem, coming down out of heaven from God . . . and I heard a loud voice from the throne saying, "Now the dwelling of God is with men, and he will live with them. They will be his people, and God himself will be with them and be their God. He will wipe every tear from their eyes. There will be no more death or mourning or crying or pain, for the old order of things is passed away" (Rev. 21:1–4, NIV).

A Concluding Perspective

For an honest and comprehensive perspective on human beings, it is necessary for theology and psychology to talk to each other and mutually illumine the anthropology with which each is dealing. The result is a reconstruction of each perspective and a more complete and sound understanding of the terminology that express the human condition in society and before God.

The concept of sin in its distorted form does not adequately reflect the biblical notion of human disorder. It is timebound, reductionistic, and primarily juridical in meaning and tone. It is not the primary biblical metaphor for our human predicament but instead disease, failure, ignorance, and covenant breaking are dominant images. In our day the metaphor of sin must be enriched. It is not exegetically permissible to cast legalistically superficial formulations when we speak of error, judgment, guilt, expiation, and justification. We must make way for the Bible's full meaning, that we are orphans who need to be adopted into the household of God.

The problem with sin is confirmed when we bring the insights of psychology to bear upon the matter. It is clear that we are bound by our distorted and inadequate natures, preset in our dysfunction by sickness at every level of our being: genetic and biochemical limitation, cognitive and affective pathology, social and cultural bias, and volitional and spiritual bondage. Both Scripture and psychology emphasize this range of our sickness. Both agree that the ultimate remedy for this condition is given full meaning in the metaphor of *healing*. The prophets speak regularly in this way, and Isaiah announces the impending arrival of the suffering Servant "by whose wounds we are healed" (53:5).

A superficial understanding of the human predicament is counterproductive to healing; it only increases human anxiety and moral burden. We force upon humans greater despair, defensiveness, regression, and unconscious sublimation, all of which are natural reactions to judgment and condemnation. The metaphor of sickness contributes a dynamically constructive dimension to the notion of sin. It sets human disorder in the context of grace. It also holds up the seriousness of that disorder in a manner that cannot readily be rationalized into superficial notions of legalistic transgressions. Moreover, the metaphor of sickness invites a realistic remedy, a formula of cooperation with God who embraces us unconditionally. It moves toward the notion of redemptive growth and healing as a divinely ordered process for our lives in Christ. It frees us to see our redemptive possibilities as we mature through instruction and guidance, and grow from the pain of acknowledging the inevitable consequences of our orphaned condition and sinful behavior.

A superficial concept of sin is too optimistic about the human condition and too pessimistic about the redeeming intent and function of God's grace. God intends not merely judgment and forgiveness but the healing of our generic disease and craziness. He invites us to grow, not merely to shape up. The biblical concept of sickness can help us to appropriate these truths, making our concept of human sin and our understanding of God's grace more profoundly adequate to the healing of human failure.

5

Psychopathology and the Problem of Guilt, Confession, and Expiation

O. HOBART MOWRER

Historically, the prevailing view in literate and nonliterate societies alike has been that persons get sick in mind, soul, and perhaps even body, because of unconfessed and unatoned real guilt. This was what an earlier era called a state of "disgrace" or "sin." As a result of complicated historical reasons, this view has, in our time, fallen into disrepute. The church, badly weakened by internal strife and by its injudicious opposition to science, quietly relinquished its traditional claim to competence in the domain of the sick soul. It unprotestingly accepted the emphasis of nineteenth-century psychiatry on constitutional and biochemical factors.

It was in this remarkable setting that psychoanalysis had its inception and rapid growth. Sigmund Freud observed in his autobiography that toward the end of the nineteenth century there were, in every large European city, "crowds of neurotics, whose number seemed further multiplied by the manner in which they hurried, with their troubles unsolved, from one physician to another."[1] The church had, in effect, turned a deaf ear to the needs of these people, and the common forms of medical and psychiatric treatment, which were predicated on a somatic conception of personality disorder, were magnificently ineffective. The situation called for a boldness which Freud supplied in the form of a clever compromise between the traditional moral view and certain medical preconceptions. Guilt, he hypothesized, was indeed a factor in neurosis, but it was a false, unrealistic, and crippling guilt which, as a result of the strict and restricting socialization of the individual, impeded the normal flow of certain instinctual energies, notably those of sex and aggression. So the psychoanalytic physician set out to cure neurotic individuals by championing the rights of the body in opposition to society and the moral order, which were presumed to be unduly harsh and arbitrary.

There was, of course, no lack of individuals who were willing to be saved by this plausible and pleasant philosophy—and who were willing to pay handsomely for it. Both patients and practioners of the art were assured, but now the day of reckoning is upon us. Our mental hospitals are full of persons who have had this new form of treatment and who have not profited from it. In the group, which includes erstwhile therapists and the general public alike, there is growing disillusionment and alarm. Once again we are in a period of sober reappraisal, and it is the purpose of this chapter to suggest one way of rethinking the problem which, although in some respects very costly, nevertheless promises a form of redemption more radical and generally more applicable than anything we have known in the recent past.

As the title of this chapter implies, it is our plan to consider, first, the possibility that in psychopathology guilt is real rather than illusory ("delusional"). Then we shall explore the correlative proposition that the aim of communication and self-disclosure in the therapeutic situation is not mere understanding and insight (in the Freudian sense of these terms) but a changed and repentant view of oneself. Finally we shall examine evidence for believing that, however necessary they may be, contrition and confession alone are not enough to restore psychic and moral

1. Sigmund Freud, *Autobiography* (New York: W. W. Norton, 1935), 27.

equilibrium and must be followed by meaningful, active forms of atonement or restitution.

Guilt Is Real

Freud held that, as a result of an overly intensive socialization, some individuals develop such a great fear of their sexual and hostile feelings that, eventually, they deny these feelings access to consciousness. It is the alarm which the ego feels when these impulses clamor for recognition and expression (the danger Freud called the "return of the repressed") that generates the characteristic neurotic effects of depression, anxiety, and panic. In 1948, this writer hypothesized that in neurosis it is actually the individual's conscience that has been repudiated and repressed rather than his instincts.[2] This shifted the emphasis from Freud's impulse theory of neurosis to a guilt theory. Actually, as is now evident, this position had been anticipated by Arvid Runestam, Anton T. Boisen, and Wilhelm Stekel,[3] and it now seems to be gaining steadily in acceptance. However, the doctrine of repression, upon which the difference in opinion here hinges, is a subtle one and not easily amenable to objective verification, so the issue has remained a debatable one.

There is another way of putting the problem which makes it more immediately researchable. According to Freud and his followers, neurotics are in trouble, not because of anything actually wrong that they have *done*, but merely because of things that they would *like* to do but, quite unrealistically, are afraid to do. By contrast, the view presented here is that in neurosis and functional psychosis individuals have committed tangible misdeeds, which have remained unacknowledged and unredeemed, and thus their anxieties have a realistic social basis and justification.

So conceived, the difference between the two positions can be empirically studied with some precision. According to the Freudian view, the neurotic should have a history of something like

---

2. O. Hobart Mowrer, *Learning Theory and Personality Dynamics* (New York: Ronald, 1950).

3. Arvid Runestam, *Psychoanalysis and Christianity* (Rock Island, Ill.: Augustana, 1932); Anton T. Boisen, *Explorations of the Inner World* (New York: Harper, 1936); Wilhelm Stekel, *Techniques of Analytical Psychotherapy* (New York: Liveright, 1938).

saintliness, whereas, according to our other position, the neurotic should have a record (albeit a carefully concealed one) of actual and incontestable misconduct and perversity. The issue should, by all means, be submitted to systematic investigation on a scale corresponding to its significance. I confess that, for myself, I am already persuaded what the results will be: Sin and emotional sickness are no strangers to each other, and it is only by flagrant disregard for the clinical facts that one can imagine that neurotic and functionally psychotic individuals have been socialized too thoroughly and are the victims of an unduly severe, oppressive morality. While no evidence cited will be sufficient to convince anyone holding a strongly contrary view, it will be accepted here as typical of a much larger body of facts which justify further consideration of the view that mental illness is a social and moral illness and, in the final analysis, that it is capable of remediation only along social and moral lines.

Guilt, Remorse, and Confession

If it is true that emotionally ill persons are typically guilty persons, that is, persons with *real* guilt rather than mere guilt *feelings*, the question very naturally arises as to what can be done to alleviate such a state of affairs. Everyone apparently has an intuitive compulsion to admit, or to confess, his or her guilt to others, but this is a very painful act and is likely to occur only under great urgency. Dramatic instances of confession, and the conflict it involves, could be given, but space does not permit it.

Despite the biblical exhortation that an honest confession is good for the soul, there is reason to doubt that its benefit is unconditional and necessarily enduring. One wonders how much, in the long run, is really accomplished by confessing only to one's therapist. What good does it do to confess your past errors to someone who is going to be as secretive about them as you have been? This private confession is not the way for a person to achieve social redefinition of personality and true redemption. Just as the offense has been against society, that is, against the laws of humankind and God, so, one might argue, the confession and forgiveness must be as broad as the sin itself.

One of the "critical incidents" collected by Raymond J. Corsini and Stanley W. Standal[4] bears directly on this question. A married woman consults a psychiatrist with complaints of depression and with obsessive thoughts that she might injure her young daughter. After desultory talk during the course of several interviews had revealed nothing but an exemplary life, the psychiatrist confronted the patient, almost roughly, with the logical incongruity between her symptoms and what she had told him about herself. With great effort she then admitted to a surprising and particularly degrading perversion, but there was no dramatic therapeutic gain. In fact, the report ends with a comment by the psychiatrist to the effect that the patient is "still in treatment."

One is prompted to wonder what would happen, in situations of this kind, if the confession took a more public form. Fortunately, we have something of an answer in a case which has been reported briefly by Anton T. Boisen:

> The patient in question was a man of thirty-eight years who was brought to the hospital in a severely agitated condition. He thought he had committed the unpardonable sin and that something was going to happen to his wife and children. He would not, therefore, let them out of his sight. He thought a world war was impending and when asked what part he was to have in this war, he replied, "A little child shall lead them." Obviously, he was the little child.
>
> The record of his life was that of a well-meaning, friendly, likeable person who before his marriage, and even afterward, had been sexually promiscuous. What troubled him most was an affair with a woman some ten years older than himself, clearly a mother substitute. There had been two abortions, for which he was responsible. She had died of carcinoma. He blamed himself for her death and the disturbance began shortly thereafter.
>
> The first symptom was heavy drinking. This continued until he lost his job. Following this, he suffered a depression and stopped drinking. Then he developed the idea that the Odd Fellows were out to get him because he had violated the oath he took when he joined them. For several months he was obsessed with ideas of persecution. He reached the point where he went to the police with a request for a permit to carry a gun in order to protect himself from his enemies. He then became finally so disturbed that he confessed to his wife, telling her of his sexual transgressions.

4. Stanley W. Standal and Raymond J. Corsini, *Critical Incidents in Psychotherapy* (New York: Prentice-Hall, 1959), 39–41.

This confession she took in good spirit, but in spite of that fact he became more and more agitated. The idea came that something was going to happen to her and that he had to carry the weight of the world on his small shoulders. Commitment then became necessary. In the hospital he showed intense anxiety. He was sure of only one thing, that things were not what they seemed. He was also deeply aroused religiously. It is not necessary for our purpose to recount his subsequent history beyond reporting that within a couple of months he made an excellent recovery and now, after nearly thirty years, there has been no further trouble. He is at present a successful contractor and his family is prosperous and happy.

After noting that this man's guilt was real and grievous, Boisen then asks:

Why now the increased agitation following the confession to his wife? Such a question is in order. The answer is clear. The emotional disturbance was not the result but the *precondition* of the confession. In his normal state of mind confession would have been impossible. But the profound emotion forced the confession, just as nature's healing power produces a boil or an abscess and then lets the poison matter out. In this case, as in others of the same type, the disturbance brought about a certain degree of socialization. It got rid of pretense and hypocrisy and put the sufferer in a position to be *accepted for what he really was*. And if it took some time for this powerful emotion to subside, that is hardly to be wondered at.[5]

All this is eminently reasonable, but does it not overlook another possibility? Voluntary confession of a legal crime may soften the ensuing punishment, but it does not abrogate it. So may we not assume that confession of an immorality likewise ends the matter? In Boisen's case I conjecture that the period of hospitalization was dynamically necessitated by the confession. This man, probably with human beings generally in like situations, felt that accounts could not be righted until he had, as we often say, "taken his medicine" and paid for his past misdeeds.

---

5. Anton T. Boisen, "Religious Experience and Psychological Conflict," *American Psychologist* 13 (1958): 568–70.

Can it be that we do not properly perceive this function of the mental hospital and hospitalization?

Beyond Confession to Restitution

Does mere confession of a legal crime absolve one from all further responsibility or punishment? Suppose that ten years ago I committed a murder and was never caught or even suspected. But as time passes, my own knowledge of the act becomes increasingly oppressive and I finally go to the local police and say, "Do you remember a man by the name of Joe Smith who was mysteriously murdered a few years ago? Well, I thought you might like to know that I killed him." What would then happen? Would the police say, "How interesting! We often wondered what happened to that fellow. Drop in again sometime." Obviously not! I would be taken into custody, would have to stand trial, and, if properly convicted, would be sentenced to what was deemed appropriate punishment.

Is the moral law less demanding than the civil and criminal codes? Does conscience have less rectitude than a court? Unless we can answer this question affirmatively, it follows that in the moral realm, no less than in law, confession is not enough and must be accompanied by restitution. This possibility has been generally neglected in our time and may account for widespread confusion and misdirected therapeutic and redemptive effort. Psychologist and psychiatrists have stressed the importance of insight rather than personal guilt and repentance, and even the church has preached what Dietrich Bonhoeffer has called the doctrine of "cheap grace," which he holds is no grace at all.[6]

Can it be that, lacking formal (institutional) recognition of the need for atonement following sin, modern men and women commonly and unconsciously make use of the stigma, disgrace, and suffering connected with being "crazy" and hospitalized? Boisen[7] has referred to the insane as the *self*-condemned, and to this we might add that they are also the *self*-sentenced. Depression is manifestly a form of self-inflicted suffering, and it has often been suspected that the reason why electroconvulsive shock treatment

---

6. Dietrich Bonhoeffer, *The Cost of Discipleship* (New York: Macmillan, 1948), 45–47.
7. Boisen, *Explorations of the Inner World*, 173.

may speed the recovery of depressed persons is that it aids the work of self-punishment. Certainly it is not uninstructive that even untreated depression tends to run its course, that the prospect of recovery from any one "attack" is always good but that recurrences are statistically likely; hence the diagnosis of "cyclothymia." Thus a depression looks very much like an act of "serving time," comparable to what happens in such other places of penance as penitentiaries where legally convicted offenders are sent. In other instances when one has "paid his debt to society" he is again free (of prison in the one case, of depression in the other), and the question of whether an individual will have one or more later depressions or will be cured depends (in much the same way as does the reformatory action of prison) upon whether he has really connected crime and punishment.

But what of schizophrenia? Here the likelihood of spontaneous remission (getting "out" or being "free") is not nearly so great, and many students of the problem suspect a deeper malignancy—tainted heredity, disordered metabolism, or the like. Can it be that schizophrenia is no less a moral disorder than is depression but that in the one case the individual is still running, hiding, and denying, whereas in the other case the individual admits his wrong at least unconsciously and accepts the justice of suffering? In Boisen's case, which had such a favorable outcome, we have an individual who showed an admixture of depressive and schizoid reactions. Apparently much depends, with respect to recovery, on whether one or the other gains the ascendancy. As Boisen has elsewhere pointed out, those persons who react to personality crises by becoming resentful and bitter and who blame others rather than themselves, are well on the way to a permanently paranoid adjustment with a very poor prognosis.[8] But when the individuals can blame themselves and see their predicament as one for which they are largely responsible and about which they can do something toward changing, their prospects of recovery—and of personal transformation—are much brighter.

Toward which of these courses is would-be therapeutic endeavor usually directed? How often we have tried to get the neurotic or psychotic (shall we say the sinful?) individual to see that his difficulties stem from sources outside his own ego or self—

8. Ibid.

from a too-strict superego, from unreasonable tyrannical parents, or from a "sick society." And how often we have, perhaps unwittingly, pushed the individual in the very direction that leads to destruction rather than salvation.

Conclusion

Perhaps in the twentieth century secular psychotherapy has already rediscovered one ancient religious truth and is on the verge of discovering another. Perhaps one of the reasons why classical psychoanalysis, with its cardinal emphasis upon "free association," so often makes a painful and productive start and then trails off into years of dull and unprofitable talk is that it does not help the analysand to move from free association (confession) to atonement, except that the financial sacrifice which analysis usually entails provides at least a temporary or symptomatic form of it. Perhaps the rest of the century will be well spent if we do nothing more than learn how, once again, to use meaningful and effective restitution as a regular and expected concomitant of confession (as in the Book of Leviticus in the Old Testament). Perhaps there are both individually and socially more constructive forms of self-punishment and atonement than incarceration in a mental hospital.

6

O. Hobart Mowrer: A Psychological and Theological Critique

JOHN V. GILMORE, JR.

O. Hobart Mowrer has a basic presupposition which underlies all his writings on psychology and religion. He says, "I cannot conceive a sound theology which is not congruent with a sound psychology; and the assumption that the two can be significantly divergent has surely been one of the most disruptive cultural elements in modern time."[1] It is always nice to be able to agree on basics, and this writer, too, embraces Mowrer's thesis. But this thesis is not the point in question. The issue really concerns the "soundness" of Mowrer's conception of both psychology and theology.

The purpose of this chapter will be to present an analysis and critique of Mowrer's psychology and theology concerning the topics of guilt, confession, and restitution.

Mowrer and Freud

Mowrer's psychology is best understood in light of Freud's writings since Mowrer essentially formulated his theory in re-

---

1. O. Hobart Mowrer, *The New Group Therapy* (Princeton: Van Nostrand, 1964), 145.

action to Freudianism. Classical Freudianism has held that neurosis is caused by an incapacitating false sense of guilt. This false guilt can be elicited by either mere temptation to do "forbidden" things, or feelings of shame for having done certain things which are actually not wrong but natural and innocent. In either case, the person, Freud held, is "too good"; he has moral standards for himself which are unrealistically rigid and demanding. Hence, psychotherapy ought not only to help the person gain insight into such unconscious mechanisms of false guilt and oppose the forces of repression, but also aid the person in beginning to express whatever impulses he feels.

It is this psychological position with which Mowrer quite strongly disagrees in practically all of his later writings. The real problem in neurosis, according to Mowrer, is not that one's standards are too high, but that one fails or refuses to live up to such standards. Mowrer posits that for humans "morality is a vital, relevant, and enduring concern,"[2] and he understands neurosis to be caused by the repudiation and repression of one's conscience, not one's instincts. The neurotic person does not have too much guilt; rather, he has too little guilt in the sense that he does not allow his guilt feelings to influence his actions.[3] The neurotic's basic trouble is that he has trangressed common moral principles. Not only has he broken such principles, but he has also repressed this guilt out of fear of social disapproval.

Freud's theory of neurosis is essentially an impulse theory, whereas Mowrer's theory is essentially a guilt theory. Freud says that neurosis is caused by one's having repressed evil wishes regarding acts he would commit if he dared, whereas Mowrer says that neurosis comes as a result of one's having committed certain acts and wishing he had not. The "primal pathogenic act" according to Freud is repression, the exclusion from consciousness of instinctual impulses whose gratification has been harshly punished in the past. On the contrary, the "primal pathogenic act," according to Mowrer, is the expression of such impulses. Freud maintains that neurosis is an "illness" created by harsh socialization, whereas Mowrer maintains that neurosis is created by the

2. O. Hobart Mowrer, "The Problem of Good and Evil Empirically Considered," *Zygon* 4 (1969): 301.
3. O. Hobart Mowrer, "Some Philosophical Problems in Mental Disorder and Its Treatment," *Harvard Educational Review* 23 (1953): 117–27.

person alone. In psychoanalytic terms, the neurotic conflict for Freud is between the id and ego as a result of a dominating superego, whereas the neurotic conflict for Mowrer is between the superego and ego as a result of the dominating id.

According to both Freud and Mowrer, neurosis is a moral struggle.[4] Freud asserts that this struggle is spurious and wasteful and should be analyzed away. Mowrer asserts that this struggle is valid and worthwhile and must be consciously responded to in order to bring healing. In colloquial terms, Freud views the neurotic as making mountains out of molehills, whereas Mowrer views the neurotic as trying to make molehills out of mountains.

Guilt

Mowrer defines guilt as "the fear a person feels *after* having committed an act which is disapproved of by the significant others in his life, before that act is detected or confessed. Guilt, in short, is the fear of being found out and punished."[5] Mowrer argues that guilt is real and is caused by a history of hidden serious misconduct. In contrast to this viewpoint, much of modern pastoral counseling has tended to emphasize guilt feelings, believing with Freud that one should not feel guilty about anything. But Mowrer has set himself against this psychoanalytic viewpoint, choosing to stress that one's anguish comes from unacknowledged and unatoned *real* guilt. Indeed, Mowrer views the neurotic person as "serving time" and blaming himself for his wrongdoing.[6]

Mowrer's contention that guilt is real, not merely feeling and "false," necessitates that there must be some objective criteria for right and wrong actions. Mowrer breaks the psychoanalytic tradition which emphasizes ethical neutrality and says that sin must be taken seriously. He dismisses the various objections to the doctrine of sin: objections such as that it cannot be defined, that it is culturally relative, that it is an unscientific concept, that it is superstition, and that such absolutes are ridiculous.[7] He says

4. Mowrer, *New Group Therapy*, 227.
5. Ibid., 226.
6. O. Hobart Mowrer, *The Crisis in Psychiatry and Religion* (Princeton: Van Nostrand, 1961), 100.
7. O. Hobart Mowrer, "Some Constructive Features of the Concept of Sin," *Journal of Counseling Psychology* 7 (1960): 185–88.

that people do not talk themselves into sin; rather, they act them-selves into sin.

Mowrer's affirmation of the doctrine of sin raises the question of whether or not he affirms the theological tenet of original sin. His response to this question is:

> I do not believe in Original Sin in the formal theological sense; but I do believe that man is originally a sinner, in the sense that by their very nature rules invite violation, and everyone has to do a certain amount of rule-violating before he "grows up" enough to see the "wisdom of the ages."[8]

He says elsewhere that "although we may not believe in the for-mal doctrines of Original Sin and the Substitutionary Atone-ment, the inescapable fact seems to be that man is an original and recurrent sinner and always will be."[9] Mowrer believes that strong forces propel one toward both virtue and evil. While he does not specify what these "forces" are, he affirms that "all men have the *capacity* for both good and evil."[10]

While Mowrer's emphasis on guilt is certainly theologically sound, he has defined sin as essentially a social transgression. Guilt is always understood as an action against certain social norms. Hence, what act actually qualifies for being sinful, it would seem, must always be culturally relative. Man's conscience becomes socially defined. The "good life" for Mowrer is confor-mity to the moral standards and values of one's society. He de-fends this definition in the following way:

> All of us live and function in some sort of social group. And a group is not just a random aggregate of individuals. It is a *system*, an agreed-upon way of doing things, a way of solving certain problems which calls for short-term sacrifices for long-term satisfactions and gains. In other words, a social system is always, in this sense, a *moral system*. . . . If one is functioning in a given social system, then one is honor-bound to "play the game," as prescribed in the sys-tem. Or, if one *must* deviate from it, to do so openly, honorably, and take the stipulated consequences of such disobedience, or else leave the system.[11]

8. Mowrer, *New Group Therapy*, 228.
9. Mowrer, "Problem of Good and Evil," 301–2.
10. Ibid., 302.
11. O. Hobart Mowrer, "Science, Sex, and Values," *Personal and Guidance Journal* 42 (1964): 751.

While rules are certainly necessary for the common good, Mowrer has erred in assuming that guilt in relationship to one's fellow man is the only sin. A corollary of Mowrer's position would seem to be that there is no sin in relationship to God and no universal standard of righteousness. However, it would seem necessary to affirm such a universal standard of righteousness if the word *sin* is to be relevant. Mowrer somehow affirms that man is a sinner yet not an original sinner in the sense of having sinned against an objective standard of righteousness. But the question must be raised as to how Mowrer can affirm man's propensity to sin without affirming either an explanation for such a propensity or a standard against which sin gains meaning.

Sin is more adequately defined as a lack of conformity to the moral law of God in being or action (Rom. 1:32; 2:12–14; 4:15). Paul says sin "is not imputed where there is no law" (Rom. 5:13b NASB), and John describes sin as "lawlessness" (1 John 3:4). Sin, then, is defined through the law and its elucidation of the will of God, "for through the law comes the knowledge of sin" (Rom. 3:20b NASB). Only in relation to the law does sin have substance and meaning, the law being the means by which a man realizes that he has come short of the will of God (Rom. 7:7–12). The basic sin is rejection of God, and every person is born under this power of sin and is inherently corrupt in his very being; sin is much more than merely a matter of rule violation and subsequent concealment. As Jeremiah says, "The heart is more deceitful than all else and is desperately sick; who can understand it?" (Jer. 17:9 NASB).

Therefore, Mowrer is open to the criticism that he is emphasizing socialization and conformity to communal standards to the exclusion of God's perfect righteousness that transcends culture and community. This notion results in a legalistic view of religion where religion is merely the servant of society, and the term *God* becomes equivalent to the idealized objective of the socialization process. But Christianity is not to be formed relative to society; rather, society is to be influenced by the righteous standards of God. As Paul said, Christians are not to be conformed to the world but are to be transformed by the renewing of their minds through the power of God that they might exercise a redemptive influence on the world (Rom. 12:1–2).

Furthermore, Mowrer seems to be advocating essentially a

pharisaical kind of religion where sole emphasis is to be placed on rules, self-perfection, and social conformity. But sin, as discussed above, is much more all-pervasive than mere acts.

Mowrer must also be criticized for assuming that all mental illness is due to repression of conscience. That is a terribly oversimplified viewpoint. Many people have serious emotional problems, not because of what they have done but because of what others have done to them. Mowrer seems to fail to recognize explicitly such a possibility. There are certainly many people who have been so victimized by their environment that to plead with them to accept personal responsibility for their actions and to confess their sins would amount to a travesty.

Much of Mowrer's shortsightedness is due to his claim that the church has fostered a wrong conception of God as being "out there." Rather, he says, it is much more accurate to think of God as "*something in here,* a part of our own selves and innermost experience."[12] Mowrer has lost any view of the transcendence of God and has made him solely a principle that is immanent and related specifically to conscience. In fact, he reduces faith in God to faith in conscience: "Can it be that we have lost faith in God because we have *lost faith in conscience?*"[13] Because God is mostly related to conscience, repression of conscience comes to be equated with the repression of God himself. Hence, Mowrer states that "in neurosis and psychosis the afflicted individual is in a moral and spiritual crisis, and that in no other circumstances does the experience of God become such a vivid reality."[14] In other words, Mowrer implies that God manifests himself most clearly in mental disorders!

It is true, of course, that every person has at least some knowledge of God's existence, glory, power, and righteousness; a general revelation of God's being is rooted, at least in part, in human consciousness (Rom. 2:14–15). Every human being has, by virtue of his humanity, a certain sense of right and wrong based on a general, though not a specific or complete, knowledge of God's standards of righteousness. It must also be agreed that neurotic "disease" ought to be viewed as basically helpful and realistic in the sense that it is a telltale sign that something is wrong. How-

12. Mowrer, *Crisis in Psychiatry and Religion,* 37.
13. Ibid., 37.
14. Ibid., 79.

ever, it is certainly a mistaken view of God to assume that he is only wrath; he is also loving (1 John 4:8, 16), faithful (1 Thess. 5:24), merciful (Luke 6:36), and good (Mark 10:18), just to name a few of his attributes. God also makes himself known to humankind in many different ways, including through creation (Ps. 19:1–6), the incarnation (Col. 2:9), and the Scripture (2 Tim. 3:16–17). In general, Mowrer seems to have little appreciation for faith in God as a personal, living relationship between a human being and Himself.

Confession

Closely tied to Mowrer's viewpoint on guilt is his position on confession. In fact, he argues that the repression of conscience is always preceded by deception of others. It is typical, he says, for one to want to conceal his wrongdoing, but this secrecy is self-defeating because it separates him from others. Moreover, he argues "that one's personality is, in truth, more importantly defined and structured by what is unknown, inward, secret about him than by what is known."[15] Because of the determinative nature of secrets, as long as a person lives under the shadow of real and unacknowledged guilt, he cannot accept himself, and healing cannot occur. In fact, Mowrer maintains that it "is doubtful that recovery without loss of 'privacy' is *ever* possible."[16]

Since the defense mechanism of suppression is central in Mowrer's theory of neurosis development, it is only logical that he view therapy as taking place only at great personal sacrifice to the client, namely, through self-revelation and deep contrition. Quoting Sidney Jourard, he states that "no man can acknowledge his real self to himself, that is, know himself, except as an outcome of disclosing himself to another person."[17] Mowrer maintains that healing and redemption depend much more upon what one says about oneself to significant others than upon what others, no matter how highly trained, say to him. Mowrer borrows a theme from Dietrich Bonhoeffer who says that sin demands to have a man by himself, isolated from others in the community. He believes that it is the act of confession that coun-

15. Mowrer, *New Group Therapy,* 70.
16. Ibid., 87.
17. Ibid., 230.

teracts this trend toward alienation from oneself, others, and God.

Confession, however, must be conducted openly in order to reap its intrapsychic and psychological benefits. Mowrer argues that confession done privately to a professional does not solve a patient's problem. Private confession only perpetuates the secrecy problem, since the professional person is only going to be as secretive about the patient's sins as the patient already is! Such "confidentiality" confounds the patient's existing privacy, withdrawal, denial, and repression. Private confession does not alleviate fears of being found out, and one should not expect much healing to occur if the individual continues to live a lie with the people who really are significant to him. Mowrer affirms that having failures known by significant others is the powerful corrective needed to change behavior. In other words, the individual must confess to those significant others whose knowledge of the sins is most dreaded. It is at this point that Mowrer recommends the practice of group confession according to the Alcoholics Anonymous scheme which he admires so much. In such a process, one admits not bad feelings but what has made the bad feelings.

The alternative to open confession is to continue to deceive the significant others. In this instance, Mowrer accurately points out that everyone has an intuitive compulsion to confess guilt and to be authentic with others; hence, the truth of one's sin will likely involuntarily burst forth into the open at some later, and perhaps most inopportune, time.

It is regarding the practice of group confession that Mowrer takes issue with the Christian church. The church, he says, started out as a small-group movement characterized by a degree of mutual self-disclosure ("exomologesis"). He claims that following the Council of Nicaea such confession began to take place privately, and by the end of the twelfth century self-disclosure before a small group had disappeared completely. The Catholic Church, according to Mowrer, has always correctly emphasized the significance of guilt by holding to the importance of contrition, confession, and penance, but vitiated the mental health benefits of such actions by having the sinner confess to a neutral third party, the priest, and by making the central aim of such actions entirely otherworldly, in the context of eternal salvation or damnation. In Mowrer's opinion, the Reformation, by emphasizing the doctrines of justification by faith and the substitutionary atonement, failed to guide men to real strength and redemption by "sealing" confession even more tightly than was characteristic of Catholicism. The format was changed from secrecy, in the confessional booth, to silence, which, according to Mowrer, was tantamount to rejecting confession altogether.[18] Divine forgiveness rather than human reconciliation was emphasized.

Mowrer is correct in contending for the importance of confessing sins to one another; this practice has good biblical warrant (James 5:16). However, he must be questioned for his advocacy of small groups of confession where those uninvolved with one's wrongdoing become privy to such actions. While confession of sins to those who already know about them does bring relief to all concerned, hanging out dirty laundry only poisons the thoughts of others. On the other hand, if the circle of confession is only as wide as the circle of knowledge, such confession of sins enables the person to receive the grace (that is, the desire and power) to change his ways. Such radical openness and transparency with significant others is not only "the most effective means of 'treatment,' but also . . . the best form of *prevention*, as a *way of life*."[19]

However, Mowrer is to be criticized for assuming that confession to God is insufficient. He contends that people usually *do not* confess to God very openly, but "very, very privately, in which event confession to God becomes a dangerous *substitute* for the more direct and painful kind of honesty."[20] In fact, he offers his own paraphrase of 1 John 4:20: " 'For he who is not open with his brother whom he has seen cannot be open with God, whom he has not seen.' "[21] However, Mowrer must be faulted for undervaluing the fact that confessing one's sins to God and receiving divine forgiveness is not cheap and easy; on the contrary, it requires surrender. The most powerful therapeutic idea in the world is the realization of God's forgiveness.

Human beings need divine as well as human forgiveness. It is

18. O. Hobart Mowrer, "Alcoholics Anonymous and the 'Third' Reformation," *Religion in Life* 34 (1965): 383–97.
19. Mowrer, *New Group Therapy*, 90.
20. Ibid., 173.
21. Ibid., 72.

not accurate to reduce confession either to a strictly horizontal level, as Mowrer wishes, or to a strictly vertical level, as Mowrer contends the Reformers desired. Both kinds of confession are necessary, and both serve a theological and psychological purpose.

Restitution

Mowrer believes that it is inadequate simply to confess sin and be assured of cleansing and healing. He contends that both conventional religion and secular psychiatry have held out for cheap, easy solutions to neurosis, religion promising divine forgiveness that is merely to be had for the asking and psychiatry promising insight and understanding that only need be purchased by the hour. Confession, according to Mowrer, can bring only transitory relief without a permanent cure. Mere openness is not enough; a neurotic person needs to undertake some activity of restitution to effect atonement and expiation of guilt.[22] Mowrer believes that no one ever talks himself out of sin; hence, there must be some "confession in action." Mowrer affirms that "it is easier to *act* yourself into a new way of thinking than to *think* yourself into a new way of acting."[23] Therefore, the neurotic person must be helped to undertake a program of service, self-discipline, and meaningful sacrifice. Mowrer says that it is primarily because of the Protestant Reformation that the church lost an appropriate emphasis on good works and left mankind with the ability to experience guilt without any personal resource for alleviating it. However, Mowrer contends that "(a person) is also capable of creativity and originality in finding ways of extricating himself from sin and working out his own salvation."[24]

How does Mowrer recommend such restitution be undertaken? In one of his articles on Alcoholics Anonymous Mowrer recommends a two-step process of personal healing.[25] First, the person is to admit his own past wrongdoings and to make steadfast efforts at restitution. Second, the individual is to engage in a program of "foregiveness," that is, an effort to give of his time and

---

22. Mowrer, *Crisis in Psychiatry.*
23. Mowrer, *New Group Therapy,* 68.
24. Mowrer, "Problem of Good and Evil," 302.
25. Mowrer, "Alcoholics Anonymous."

concern to others who are in need before others have done anything for him. This type of life-style is better than traditional forgiveness in which an individual has to get something from another. According to Mowrer, his program provides a security and strength which others have not conferred and which others cannot take away. A person, then, is freed from his neurosis, not by what others say to him, but by what he does for others and ultimately for his own benefit. The individual is to recommit himself to society by compensating for his transgressions with new actions that enhance the social structure instead of violating it.

The program that Mowrer recommends sounds very much like the life-style of accumulating credits that he suggests in one of his books.[26] In a sense, of course, Mowrer is right in stressing the importance of good works; they are important. Theologically, however, Mowrer is to be criticized for advocating a thoroughgoing theology of works which the Reformation so strongly rejected. Mowrer tries to draw a sharp dichotomy between Paul and James by saying, in essence, that Paul is irrelevant and James alone has "true religion" (James 1:27). Historically he is advocating a theology of good works that is more extreme than Pelagianism, which at least recognized the need for the assistance of God's grace. At one point Mowrer argues that, even though it is not always possible to atone for some sins "in kind," we can *try*—and if we persevere long enough, knock hard enough, the door eventually opens."[27] Mowrer seems to be advocating an excessive scrupulosity that is not healthy psychologically. It is also true that Mowrer is advocating that people undertake a program of good works, not for altruistic reasons, but mostly from selfish motives.

Mowrer, of course, deplores the doctrine of the substitutionary atonement precisely because he claims the work of restitution must be done by the person himself, not for him by someone else. But Mowrer fails to understand that to be justified in Christ by faith is significant precisely because it costs nothing; it is a free gift! This fact does not make the substitutionary atonement of Christ cheap. Instead, a response to Christ's work where the individual appreciates and trusts completely in that sacrificial act (apart from any human effort to work for personal justification)

26. Mowrer, *New Group Therapy,* 69–70.
27. Mowrer, *Crisis in Psychiatry,* 199.

will result in a strong cognitive dissonance. Being declared righteous without having worked for and achieved such a declaration ought to prompt good works that result from salvation in Christ, rather than works that attempt to be a means to salvation. Mowrer fails to see that faith and works are inseparable. There is no contradiction between Paul and James in the New Testament. A person's expiation is realized by confessing total dependence on God's work alone in Christ (Eph. 2:8–9). Good works, important as they are, result from such faith. Faith without works only proves that there has been no faith initially, as James himself points out in chapter 2.

PART 2

Guilt

7

Pastoral Counseling and the Problem of Guilt

LeRoy Aden

According to the Christian faith, guilt is a decisive part of the human predicament. It describes our condition before self, others, and God and indicates that we are at least partly responsible for that condition. It burdens us with a sense of judgment and condemnation and aggravates our feeling of impotence. It drives spiritually sensitive individuals to despair and impels them to find some kind of gracious refuge.

Pastoral counseling also indicates that guilt is a frequent and significant problem in the lives of troubled people. Guilt is a major ingredient in most forms of psychological disturbance and a primary factor in most forms of interpersonal estrangement. It is what we are and not just what we have done, so it becomes a decisive determinant of who we are and of who we can become. It enslaves with its subtlety, paralyzes with its pain, and drives us toward despair with its endlessness. Consequently, we often try to push it into the dark and hidden recesses of our lives—or, in a more positive vein, we face up to our powerlessness and seek help from someone beyond ourselves.

A problem of such import deserves careful study. In this chapter we want to take a close look at the experience of guilt, lifting out some of its major psychological and theological characteristics. The study will help us to recover a sense of the depth of guilt and to appreciate the interrelationship between a psychological and a theological understanding of it.

The Nature of Guilt

Paul Tillich defines anxiety as the "existential awareness of nonbeing" or, more precisely, as a "state in which a being is aware of its possible nonbeing."[1] Guilt can be defined in a parallel way, partly because it is close enough to anxiety to be called "moral anxiety." Guilt is the existential awareness of moral nonbeing or, in other words, it is a condition in which individuals are aware of negation in the moral sphere of their self-affirmation.

The actual experience of guilt seldom takes this abstract form. Instead it is usually experienced as a distressing incongruity between what I ought to do and what I have done or between who I should be and who I actually am. In other words, guilt presupposes a norm or an expectation in relation to which I am found "wanting." The norm may come from a number of different sources, specifically from society, from self, or from God, but whatever the source, guilt is a discrepancy between the ideal and the actual, a discrepancy for which I bear some real responsibility.

At its best, guilt goes beyond our failure to obey certain laws, whether internal or external, human or divine. Instead it refers basically to our failure to fulfill ourselves, to become what we are meant to be through proper relation to ourselves, to others, and, above all, to God. Guilt is primarily distorted fulfillment. David E. Roberts says that every human being finds "himself in a setting, from birth to death, wherein he is continually violating his own good nature."[2] Roberts goes on to say that the violation is not caused merely by ignorance or by physical and social influences but that it also comes from the individual's own will or power of self-determination. In this way, Roberts makes improper fulfillment a personal and basic fault in the individual.

1. Paul Tillich, *The Courage to Be* (New Haven: Yale University Press, 1962), 35.
2. David E. Roberts, *Psychotherapy and a Christian View of Man* (New York: Scribners, 1950), 107.

Actually, we need to clarify the nature of guilt in more detail, partly because we can distinguish at least three different types of guilt: rule guilt, existential guilt, and ultimate guilt. These three types of guilt may be seen more properly as three different perspectives on a single reality, the gap between what is and what ought to be. In any case, we will find the psychological theories of O. Hobart Mowrer and Sigmund Freud useful in making distinctions.

Rule Guilt

According to Mowrer, the primary cause of neurosis, humanity's basic plight, resides in what he calls "real guilt" and its subsequent denial. By real guilt Mowrer refers to the commission of "tangible social misdeeds," acts which violate the individual's particular social milieu. He equates goodness and badness with actual performance and insists that the person becomes guilty in the moment of overt rule violation. The heart of guilt, then, becomes unlawful behavior or the tangible transgression of one's social norms and taboos.

Mowrer's emphasis on actual violation is illustrated by the situation of Mrs. Demand, a thirty-five-year-old mother of two who had become pregnant out of wedlock when she was in her late teens. Because she felt unable to share her plight with her parents, she decided to terminate the pregnancy by a self-induced abortion. She completed the task with difficulty and emerged from the whole experience with a nagging sense of dis-ease:

Mrs. Demand: I just can't stand myself for what I did. And it doesn't help to have Mr. Alright [her minister] tell me it doesn't matter, that God forgives me, and since he forgives me, why can't I just forget about it? That is fine. It sounds great, but it doesn't help how I feel.

Counselor: You still feel very bad and guilty.

Mrs. Demand: Well, yes. I believe that human life is valuable, and no one has a right to take a life. And when they tell me, "That really wasn't a life. It was merely a small clump of flesh and genes," that's fine. But I did it. I took a potential life, and I did not have that right.

Mowrer's approach tends to support Mrs. Demand's tendency to locate the basic evil in her socially reprehensible behavior. Mowrer would maintain that all of her difficulties, including her personal and interpersonal troubles, can be traced back ultimately to a foul deed, for it is an actual deed that is the locus of her guilt and the source of her alienation from society. Denial of the deed does no good. Denial does not rob guilt of its destructive power but rather forces it to express the truth in clamorous symptoms of neurotic disturbance. Mrs. Demand, then, must come to acknowledge the full impact of her evil behavior. She must experience guilt for what she has actually done, for in this experience she will arrive at the threshold of the only genuine solution—the willingness to confess her foul behavior to significant others and to make appropriate restitution to the society whose rules she has violated.

Mowrer's theory represents one possible interpretation of the nature of guilt. It is a good example of what we can call rule guilt, that is, a guilt that is incurred because the individual has violated some norm or standard. Mowrer's theory has definite limitations, even from a clinical point of view. To get a more complete picture of guilt, we turn to the psychoanalytic theory of Sigmund Freud.

Existential Guilt

According to Freud, people do not begin life as moral creatures. In fact, they are decidedly amoral, consisting of various desires which seek gratification immediately and multifariously. The first modification comes in the form of a parent who disapproves of specific impulses and who therefore confronts the child with a more or less definite form of restraint. For Freud, the climax of this encounter comes when the five- or six-year-old child experiences Oedipal desires. The child longs to possess the parent of the opposite sex and, by the same token, to get rid of the parent of the same sex. The result is dramatic. Oedipal desire confronts parental law or external reality to an extent where the very existence of the child is in danger, in fantasy if not in reality.

Confronted by this threat, children gradually renounce and repress their unacceptable desires. In fact, their whole relationship with the rival parent changes from wanting to displace and get rid of him or her to wanting to emulate and be like him or her. In Freudian language, they identify with and introject the parent, so that the parent's external precepts and prohibitions gradually become the child's own. In this process, children become genuinely moral persons insofar as they internalize the demands of society as mediated through the parents and begin to judge themselves as severely as the parents did. They become self-controlled, self-repressed individuals who are, to some degree, obedient to the introjected demands of their social context.

Freud's theory goes beyond Mowrer and illuminates the nature of guilt in three important respects. First, it makes guilt an attitudinal, instead of a behavioral, matter, because it describes the occasion that leads to guilt as an internal, and not merely as an external, happening. Individuals stand against their desires and feel guilty for them, whether or not they actually carry them out. This position allows for the possibility that people are guilty because their inner lives, the center of their being is distorted and in disrelationship. Second, Freud associates guilt with a decisive event and a crucial relationship in the child's life, so that the whole struggle with morality is built into the fabric of human existence. At the same time, his theory locates the actualization of guilt in a concrete event, so that individuals themselves are responsible for their plight. For Freud, then, guilt is an individual event that takes place under the impact of universal conditions.

Third, Freud implies that guilt goes beyond rule violation and involves a violation of the individual's basic nature. For Freud, "nature" refers to libidinal sexual desires, at least in his early thought. Later he expanded his understanding of "nature" to include life instincts and death instincts, that is, pervasive desires that drive toward both the enrichment of life and the destruction of life. We do not necessarily have to agree with Freud's understanding of "nature" to benefit from his insight that guilt has to do, not just with rule violation, but more deeply with the violation of our humanity. This violation may be perpetrated against the self, the other person, or the relationship between them, but in any case it refers to an "act that contradicts the self-realization of the person as a person and drives toward disintegration."[3]

In three respects, then, Freud posits a profound understanding of the nature of guilt and seems to point to what can be called existential guilt, that is, to a basic violation of self or the other

3. Paul Tillich, *Morality and Beyond* (New York: Harper and Row, 1963), 20.

person or the relationship between them. For him, guilt becomes the distortion or the diminution of personhood.

However profound, the final value of Freud's understanding of guilt is diminished by an important flaw. While Freud sees below mere deed to humankind's basal desires, he does not make the desires themselves the fountain of guilt. In fact, he maintains that they are the original and basic part of human nature, prior to morality, so they are experienced in infancy as neither good nor bad. In Freud's technical language, "The id knows no values, no good and evil, no morality. The economic or, if you prefer, the quantitative factor, which is so closely bound up with the pleasure principle, dominates all its processes."[4] Within this framework, morality becomes an addition to human nature, and not an inextricable part of it. "We may reject the existence of an original, as it were natural, capacity to distinguish good from bad. . . . There is an extraneous influence at work, and it is this that decides what is to be called good or bad."[5] As we have seen, the "extraneous influence" refers to social laws that are internalized.

Freud's position reduces morality to a set of prohibitions and expectations which, no matter how well they are introjected, always remain extraneous to the individual's essential nature. For him, then, as for Mowrer, guilt originates in the breaking of a heteronomous law, whether internal or external. It represents a violation of a system of commands, and not a violation of the individual's inner *telos*. Contrary to this understanding of guilt, we want to acknowledge the fact that guilt runs to the deepest level of human life. It is a transgression against our very humanity on both the personal and interpersonal levels. In other words, it goes beyond mere disobedience of the law to a destructive violation of one's essential nature. It is people at war with themselves, people fulfilling themselves in faulty and deleterious ways.

Ultimate Guilt

According to theology, genuine fulfillment is possible only in relationship with God, for we cannot really actualize our created nature apart from our Creator. In fact, without God we become

4. Sigmund Freud, *New Introductory Lectures on Psychoanalysis*, trans. W. J. H. Sprett (New York: W. W. Norton, 1933), 105.

5. Sigmund Freud, *Civilization and Its Discontents*, trans. Joan Riviere (London: Hogarth, 1969), 61.

centered in ourselves, so that all our actions proceed from a corrupt center and are only egoistic attempts at self-fulfillment. This is the quintessence of faulty fulfillment and the heart of ultimate guilt. It is life revolving around itself, suffering the agony of being cut off from the Power who alone is able to sustain life and to grant genuine fulfillment. This agony—the agony of ultimate guilt—is given existential expression by a forty-year-old woman who suffered from guilt to a point where she had a temporary breakdown. When the turmoil subsided, she recorded her struggle with God or, more precisely, with the absence of God. The following is a small part of her reminiscence:

> More heart-broken than afraid, I see within that inner space of the heart, the despairing Shadow trying to "exist" without God, i.e., against God, shut up within her limitations, blind to the Life without which her very existence would not "be." This is what it means "to be by nature sinful and unclean. *There* is sin, and it literally implies Death—the Shadow, like a little ball of derived energy, exists, whirling upon itself, with its void center.

Seen theologically, ultimate guilt is sin or, to be more precise, what we are guilty of ultimately is sin. This means that guilt, like sin, is not a monolithic state but an ontological estrangement consisting of three interrelated marks. First, we are immersed in the guilt of unbelief. Unbelief is not a cognitive or an emotional reluctance to believe in the doctrines of the church but a total turning away from God, a failure to trust him or, more drastically, an active enmity against him. Second and simultaneously, our guilt is *hubris* or self-elevation. In turning from God we turn toward ourselves, making ourselves the center of life and the source of our own fulfillment. Finally, seeking this false center, we fall into concupiscence, "the unlimited desire to draw the whole of reality into"[6] ourselves. We are driven by an endless and inordinate attempt to possess the whole of life.

We have now looked at guilt from three different angles—as a violation of rules, persons, and God. While each form of guilt has its own distinct identity, each is also related to the other two. The violation of rules (rule guilt) is not simply the transgression of external prohibitions, but to the extent that the prohibitions de-

6. Paul Tillich, *Systematic Theology* (Chicago: University of Chicago Press, 1957), 2: 52.

fine the parameters within which we find genuine fulfillment, rule guilt comes close to existential guilt's violation of our humanity. And to violate our humanity is not simply to violate the self; it is also a violation of the One who created us. It is a denial of, and a transgression against, God through unbelief, *hubris*, and concupiscence.

The Burden of Guilt

Tillich says of anxiety, "It is impossible for a finite being to stand naked anxiety for more than a flash of time. People who have experienced these moments, as for instance some mystics in their visions of the 'night of the soul,' or Luther under the despair of the demonic assaults, or Nietzsche-Zarathustra in the experience of the 'great disgust,' have told of the unimaginable horror of it."[7] Psychotherapy indicates that the same thing can be said of guilt. Anyone who has experienced the power of a stricken conscience can verify the point. Miss Havelock,[8] a thirty-three-year-old woman who underwent an induced abortion after becoming pregnant out of wedlock, gives expression to the nagging nature of guilt.

> *Miss Havelock:* The worst thing of all about it was . . . that I saw what would have been my child, and I didn't know, no one ever told me, that in that short time . . . arms and a head and legs would develop . . . that it wasn't just a matter of getting rid of a thing, that it was a real human being. And no one ever told me that I'd wake up at night hearing myself cry, "I want my baby!"

> *Counselor:* This experience leaves you with a terrific sense of guilt, almost as if you killed someone.

> *Miss Havelock:* It isn't just "almost." It's exactly that I did kill someone. One night my brother was talking to some friends about his war experiences. He was telling us about the people he killed. I guess it was two or three. And then he

7. Tillich, *Courage to Be*, 39.
8. The situation of Miss Havelock is similar in many respects to the case of Mrs. Demand, but the two should not be confused.

ended by saying, "You never forget the people you kill." And then you wonder why I can't sleep at night.

Counselor: Like him, you can't forget what you did, can't get beyond the point at which you . . . killed your child.

Miss Havelock: It seems like that. (Pause) It's like I can never go past this. . . . It's just like this is some kind of gate or something. I can't cross it. I'm guilty; therefore, I'm condemned, and . . . that's it. When I first came back, I just very literally had to shut myself in my apartment, not go anywhere, not see anyone, not do anything, because if I had seen anyone . . . the desire to tell everyone, to . . . I don't know, in a sense be forgiven because I couldn't forgive myself for what I had done. I knew if I saw anyone, I'd start talking and . . . I couldn't afford to do that.

Miss Havelock is able to talk about her guilt without being devastated by it because she has been in therapy for nearly a year. This fact suggests another similarity between anxiety and guilt. Tillich points to the similarity when he says that the horror of anxiety "is ordinarily avoided by the transformation of anxiety into fear of something, no matter what."[9] A sense of guilt is often handled in the same way. Its agony is muffled by repression, by projection, by displacement, or by some other defense mechanism, so that it is often experienced indirectly as fear, hostility, sadness, or some other less threatening feeling.

When guilt is experienced as guilt, it seems to be made up of several different components. A close look at each component will help to pinpoint the burden of guilt.

A Sense of Defilement

The first component is highlighted by the experience of twenty-nine-year-old Mrs. Palmer. She went to work to ease the family's financial situation and became involved in an extramarital affair that she continued for over a year, even though she was haunted by a nagging sense of guilt. She brought the affair to an abrupt end when her mother died unexpectedly. About a month after the

9. Tillich, *Courage to Be,* 39.

funeral she became increasingly restless and confused. A "dirty, obscene name" started to go through her mind, and soon she was paralyzed psychologically by hallucinatory thoughts of death and destruction. She was terrified of death, but she was terrified even more by the thought of meeting God. Her reason illuminates the agony of guilt, however suspect it may be theologically.

> *Mrs. Palmer:* When my soul is before God, I'm afraid that the other people up there will point their fingers at me and say, "Look at her! How did she get up here? Look how dirty her soul is. She isn't worthy of heaven. There is no good in her. Who does she think she is fooling?"
>
> *Counselor:* You feel that people in heaven will condemn you?
>
> *Mrs. Palmer:* Yes, I do. All the good people up there . . . you know, all the saints, will look down on me. They'll know I am dirty, that I don't have a single good thing in me. My mother won't understand either. When she sees what I've done, she'll never be able to forgive me. She may even have nothing to do with me. (Becomes tearful) She was such a good women that she would never be able to understand me.
>
> *Counselor:* So you feel that even in death your evilness will separate you from others. You'll be all alone.
>
> *Mrs. Palmer:* Yes, all alone. All alone.

Mrs. Palmer, tortured by the thought that the "saints" in heaven will see how dirty she is, shows that guilt includes a more or less explicit feeling of being unclean or contaminated. The agony of guilt is constituted in part by the feeling that we have corrupted ourselves, that we have stained or distorted who we are or ought to be. Obviously, this unclean feeling need not take a glamorous form like the one above; it can and in counseling it often does take a more indirect form, like a vague feeling of self-disgust or a nauseous sickness in the stomach or a desperate need to be outwardly clean and orderly. Whatever its form, the feeling of corruption seems to be a universal component of the guilt experience—a conclusion that finds support in human-kind's literary and religious history whenever its preguilt state is described as a condition of innocence and its postguilt state is populated by rites of purification.

Mrs. Palmer's sense of contamination revolves around a specific act or series of acts. As we have seen, this fact is congruent with Mowrer's interpretation of guilt. While counseling indicates that a sense of defilement often inheres in an unseemly deed, it also indicates that the individual's sense of corruption resides finally in what the individual "is" rather than in what the individual "does." In fact, in later phases of counseling the corrupted deed is seen as the externalization of an internal corruption, that there is disorder in the center of one's life which manifests itself in one's outward activity. In this sense, then, guilt as a feeling of contamination is an agony that touches the core of one's being. It is the awful awareness that I have stained myself, that, as one patient put it, "I am as dung upon the face of the earth."

Out of the agony of contamination comes the need to be made clean. "Create in me a clean heart, O God, and put a new and right spirit within me."[10] The psalmist's plea penetrates to the core. The mere appearance of clean hands or noble words is not enough. Individuals who are burdened with guilt long for a clean heart, for an inner rightness that restores their innocence and makes them "whiter than snow." Nothing less than a complete renewal of their inward parts will satisfy the longing to be washed thoroughly from impurity.

A Feeling of Disloyalty

The burden of guilt is constituted by a second ingredient, namely, the feeling that one has been unfaithful or disloyal to some significant person or principle. For example, when Miss Havelock went through the abortion and saw what would have been her child, she felt that she had betrayed her unborn child and the father of the child, her family's image and expectation of her, her own self-image and self-expectation, and even her understanding of God or, more abstractly, her understanding of "the Good" and "the Decent." Miss Havelock gives expression to the anguish of being disloyal to her "better self":

10. Ps. 51:10 (RSV).

Miss Havelock: I wished a million times that I had gone through with it. (Slight pause) Funny, I . . . it's a funny thing to say, but almost from the time I saw the doctor, I lived with the horror that someday . . . under some kind of circumstance, it would happen again because it had not been meant for me to find . . . an escape as I did. I don't know exactly what my reasoning is. But it's just another occasion when I ran away. I knew what I should do, but I evaded it. I couldn't face it, and I didn't.

Counselor: And you've lived with regret ever since, wishing you had had the courage to see it through.

Miss Havelock: That's it. To be able to face things, to see it through . . . to its logical end. That's what I should have done.

Disloyalty can be a crucial and devastating part of guilt, for it usually means that the individual has been unfaithful, not just in the superficial sense of failing to do what is expected but in the deeper sense of forsaking something or somebody who is a decisive and intimate part of his or her life. In this sense, disloyalty always involves a betrayal of oneself as well as a betrayal of the other. In any case, it goes against one of the essential marks of human existence—what Andras Angyal calls the homonomous tendency of the individual "to surrender himself willingly, to seek a home for himself in and *to become an organic part of something that he conceives as greater than himself.*"[11] This tendency proceeds from the fact that individuals are not merely autonomous beings but also interpersonal beings. They are inextricably enmeshed in, and related to, realities beyond themselves, not only in the phylogenetic sense of being a member of a species but also in the more immediate sense of being a participant in a family, a society, a culture, and a cosmic order. They may give, or fail to give, themselves to any number of these transpersonal realities, but they cannot eliminate the homonomous trend as a basic and powerful striving in their lives. Being disloyal frustrates and threatens to overthrow this trend and causes noticeable pain. It represents a tearing down of homonomous commitments and is

11. Andras Angyal, "A Theoretical Model for Personality Studies," *Journal of Personality* 20, 1 (Sept. 1951), 132; emphasis added.

therefore both a possible source of guilt and a vital part of its agony.

Out of the agony of disloyalty comes the fear of being rejected and the desire to be reunited with those who have been betrayed. The psalmist experiences both possibilities and asks God to preserve them. "Cast me not away from Thy presence, and take not Thy Holy Spirit from me."[12] Even if guilty individuals do not direct their petitions to God, the anxiety of rejection and the fear of being cut off from significant others is a vital part of the agony of guilt.

The Pain of Deception

The experience of counselors is that deception and dishonesty comprise a third component of the burden of guilt. Miss Havelock illustrates this point in her struggle with memories of the past:

Miss Havelock: The most horrible part about it, the hardest thing for me is . . . having to live a lie, even to my family to whom I have never lied. They were all so concerned about me that one week when I was so terribly sick. They thought I was sick with the flu, and I couldn't tell them what was wrong. So since the beginning, it's been demanded of me that I live that lie . . . for the rest of my life. The Bible says you shall know the truth, and the truth shall make you free. They don't know how true that is . . . or to how many things it applies. I could probably find forgiveness in the hearts of every single member of my family, yet I wonder if I would still—even after that—forgive myself for what I did.

Counselor: You feel, then, that in a sense you're even living this lie in relation to yourself.

Miss Havelock: Yes, I think so. I think a great deal so, because sometimes I try to make excuses for myself by thinking that if this had not happened, things would be different. I live in a world—how shall I say it—I find myself in sort of a wishful state, a state of "ifs" or impossibilities or implausibilities, trying to undo something that has already been done.

12. Ps. 51:11 (RSV).

Miss Havelock implies that living a lie is painful for two major reasons. First, it discolors her relationship to those who are most significant to her and thus aggravates her condition of isolation and disrelation. In other words, being deceptive flies in the face of our homonomous need to be related to, and to be a genuine part of, a transpersonal reality. In fact, it puts severe qualifications on any kind of relating, for it means that we must always hang onto ourselves and never let anyone get too close. Thus we live in a world of unfreedom and shutupness or, as Miss Havelock puts it, "The Bible says you shall know the truth, and the truth shall make you free." Where the truth about oneself cannot be known there is no freedom, not even with those with whom we should be most free.

Second, being deceptive distorts our relation to ourselves. It posits a radical split in the center of our being, dividing our life into those things that can be acknowledged and those things that must be kept hidden. This situation is contrary to the second essential characteristic of human existence—the trend toward increased autonomy. According to Angyal, this trend "expresses itself in a striving of the person to consolidate and increase his self-government, in other words, to exercise his freedom and to organize the relevant items of his world out of the autonomous center of government that is his self."[13] Angyal locates the roots of this tendency in the fact that we are not passive creatures who are a mere "resultant of external forces" but that we are active initiators of many of our own functions. We are centers of self-determination who are able to act according to our own intrinsic nature and to impose our wishes upon the impinging world.

Self-deception frustrates this organismic capacity, for it creates a state within a state, a split in which a small selected part of the total personality tries to govern the whole. The agony inherent in this situation is intensified by the fact that we cannot escape some awareness of our deception. While we can cover up our dishonesty, we know in unguarded moments in the silent recesses of life that we are living a lie without the power or the courage to change it. As Miss Havelock says, "I couldn't tell them what was wrong. So since the beginning, it's been demanded of me that I live that lie . . . for the rest of my life."

13. Angyal, "Theoretical Model," 132.

The agony of dishonesty creates a need to be open and above-board, however much we may have to repress that need in order to keep our guilt hidden. Thus guilt tends to arouse in us what the psalmist says of God: "Thou desirest truth in the inward parts: therefore in the hidden part make me to know wisdom."[14] Mrs. Demand illustrates the point. At one point she tells her counselor, "I don't want to tell you what I did; I don't want anybody to know," but she goes on to say, "I'm going to have to go through it. I can't back away any longer." Underneath this struggle is the desire to "ring true," to be authentic. This desire seems to be one of the primary reasons why people go into counseling, and it is probably one of the primary reasons why they are healed in and through it.

The Sting of Judgment

In another interview, Mrs. Demand deals with her relationship to various members of her family, and in the process she points to a fourth component that often makes guilt a burden.

> *Mrs. Demand:* What would my kids think if they knew? What am I going to tell my daughter when she gets to an age where I have to talk to her? What would they say if they ever caught a fleeting glimpse of what I had been?

> *Counselor:* They would feel that you're a horrible mother?

> *Mrs. Demand:* Yeah, I guess so. They would probably never believe it . . . I mean, never believe that I could do such a thing. Oh, their whole image of me would be shattered.

> *Counselor:* I guess quite intensely you feel, "No one—not my husband, not my children, not any one—could accept me if they got a full view of what I have done, have been. They just couldn't respect me."

Mrs. Demand's reaction indicates that the prospect of being judged and rejected is a distressing part of guilt. Like components we have previously examined, its distress probably derives from the fact that our organismic need to belong to, and to be accepted by, significant others is threatened. In addition, it tends to re-

14. Ps. 51:6.

inforce an attitude we have taken toward ourselves, so the feeling of being condemned reaches an intolerable pitch. While Mrs. Demand gives phenomenological expression to the point, Paul Tillich gives ontological/psychological expression to it when he says that we stand over against ourselves and judge what we have made of ourselves. This critical self-judgment is, in relative terms, the anxiety of guilt; in absolute terms, the anxiety of self-rejection or condemnation. Tillich elaborates: "The anxiety of guilt . . . is present in every moment of moral self-awareness and can drive us toward complete self-rejection, to the feeling of being condemned—not to an external punishment but to the despair of having lost our destiny."[15]

The Despair of Lost Destiny

We have now considered four components that contribute to the existential agony of guilt. While any one of them is serious enough to cause anguish, there is a fifth ingredient that seems to be even more basic and distressing. It is the feeling that one has lost one's real self, that by fulfilling oneself in a distorted way one has forfeited the chance, maybe even the right, to become what one was meant to be. Tillich calls it the "despair of having lost our destiny."[16] Whatever the term, it is the agony of missing the mark or of being bent out of shape. Mrs. Demand struggled with this agony. Her guilt of fornication and murder stained her with the indelible feeling that she could not be—in fact that she dare not be—herself. "A lot of my problem, I know, is that I am full of life, but I've never been able to express it because it is wrong. . . . I know what I am, but I can't be it."

To lose one's destiny is agony, either prospectively or retrospectively. Angyal gives us a psychological reason why. He describes the individual as a time Gestalt, a dynamic and organized process that strives for the perfect realization of its basic nature, its system principle, as it moves through time. Concretely, this means that we have an organismic and undeniable need to shape our lives into coherent and meaningful wholes. We need to feel that we are molding our life course into something worthwhile, that we are moving toward some meaningful end-point. We may never

15. Tillich, Courage to Be, 52f.
16. Ibid., 53.

be fully aware of this concern, but it operates nevertheless, coloring our temporary and secondary activities with a final sense of responsibility for what we are making of the unique opportunity called life. Because we are both autonomous and homonomous beings, this desire for self-realization means in a very basic sense that we must feel that we are becoming real persons within a relationship of persons. Any significant deviation from this path by thought or deed can create a harsh reaction, a critical sense that we have violated our own basic nature. We are, therefore, closed in upon ourselves with only a distorted future ahead of us.

Lost destiny also creates agony from a moral viewpoint, but Angyal has already anticipated the reason. True morality is not mere obedience to the law, whether internal or external, human or divine. Instead it is "to become actually what one is essentially and therefore potentially." More precisely, it is to fulfill "the inner law of our true being, of our essential or created nature." This imperative means, above everything else, that the individual must become a "person within a community of persons."[17] Any actualization that contradicts and distorts this basic goal moves us in the direction of disintegration and plunges us into the pit of having lost our way, lost our real self.

Conclusion

What we have said in this discussion can be misleading. It dwells on the negative side of guilt; it tends to cover up the fact that guilt is part of our grandeur and is basically a positive and constructive reaction. Its positive intent is parallel to what Roberts says of the doctrine of sin: "The motive behind the doctrine of sin . . . is not to drive in a sense of despair and insufficiency just because one enjoys seeing men wriggle in agony. The motive behind it is to reach full awareness of the depth of the human problem."[18] Guilt is an alarm system that tells us that something is wrong in the moral sphere of our self-affirmation. It is our constructive and essential capacity to stand above our own concretions and to know when we posit a discrepancy between what we ought to be and what we actually are. While it does not tell us

17. Tillich, *Morality and Beyond*, 20f.
18. Roberts, *Psychotherapy and a Christian View*, 106.

specifically what is wrong (it is not primarily a cognitive experience), it does make us aware of the fact that something significant is wrong. If the warning is heeded and the appropriate action taken, its positive intent to call us back to ourselves, back to a more fulfilling and health-giving existence, is accomplished.

However positive in intent, guilt is still a burden, an unbearable anxiety. Consequently, it tends to drive us toward a solution, sometimes toward any solution. To paraphrase Tillich, the burden of guilt is usually avoided by transforming it into something else, no matter what. In chapter 10 we will explore one particular solution to guilt—our attempt to make ourselves right.

8

Psychoanalytic Contributions to the Christian View of Guilt

S. Bruce Narramore

The psychoanalytic view of guilt does not lend itself to either simplistic or dogmatic presentations. Arguments rage about the centrality of the Oedipus complex in neurosis in general and in superego development in particular. On top of this we have the ever-present problem of Sigmund Freud's views on guilt and the superego. As was so often the case, he never fully integrated all of his statements about the superego into one final statement. Thus it is difficult to present *the* psychoanalytic view of guilt.

Unfortunately, the Christian view of guilt is not much better. From New Testament times through the Reformation to the present, there have been a variety of attitudes about the role of guilt in Christian experience. It is beyond the scope of this chapter to trace the history of the concepts of conscience and guilt in Christian theology. Beside this constraint, my primary concern is with the affective side of the problem of guilt and conscience.

Given this understanding of both the psychoanalytic and Christian views of guilt, my goal is to discuss the emotion of guilt

117

as it is experienced and conceived by the person on the street, in the light of generally accepted psychoanalytic thinking. In doing this I would suggest that there are several frequent misconceptions about the nature, purpose, and origin of guilt. Psychoanalytic thinking can guide us toward a more complete and accurate view of it. Most of us are aware of the distinction between guilt as a legal, judicial, or theological concept and guilt as an emotion. Although I believe psychoanalysis has a great deal to say about guilt as a theological condition, I want to focus on guilt as an affect, as a feeling.

I feel constrained to make one disclaimer. I do not consider myself a disciple of Freud, nor do I endorse the entirety of psychoanalytic thinking. Once I set aside many preconceived notions about psychoanalytic theory and techniques, however, I found a great number of principles that fit clearly into the biblical view of persons. Some psychoanalytic concepts have stimulated me to dig more deeply into the Scripture to get beyond a typically superficial Christian view of sin, psychopathology, and guilt.

While everyone experiences guilt feelings differently, if we ask the typical conservative Christian what guilt is and what role it should play in the Christian life, we likely would get a response something like this: "For me, guilt is that feeling of badness or of having done wrong that is instilled by God (or at least triggered by him in some way) when I sin or fall short of his standards. It is a feeling that should motivate me to improve my behavior or performance to get it more in line with God's ideals." I imagine some people would go on to say that they believe that guilt also involves some kind of mental punishment for their misbehaviors. In other words, I would suggest that many Christians conceive of guilt as

1. A painful, negative emotion . . .
2. That somehow comes from God . . .
3. And is a consequence of our misbehavior . . .
4. In order to motivate us to improved behavior . . .
5. And to serve as a form of mental punishment for our sins.

This is, in no way, a theologically accurate perception, but I believe it is the "theological view" held by the typical Christian layperson. Unfortunately, I fear that it is often the view held by clergy too.

The Origin of Guilt Feelings

We can begin with one of the most basic of these questions: Do guilt feelings really come from God? I think most of us would agree that at least some guilt feelings are the product, not of God, but of early childhood experiences. Sometimes, however, those of us who work regularly with patients forget that not all people share our insights into the psychological origins of guilt. We also forget that our own insights into guilt development have come largely from a stream of psychological thinking that originated with psychoanalysis. Paul Tournier, for example, acknowledges our indebtedness to Freud when he writes:

> You are acquainted with Freud's explanation: According to him, feelings of guilt are the result of social constraint. The feelings are born in the mind of the child when his parents scold him, and are nothing other than fear of losing the love of parents who have become suddenly hostile. No one today contests the reality of this mechanism, nor the importance of Freud's discovery, which only confirms what the Bible had already told us—how much the human being needs to feel loved.[1]

He goes on to say that "we have just seen too many examples of guilt feelings aroused by the suggestion of educators and society to deny the mechanism described by Freud and his school. It is the guilt produced by fear of taboos. The question then arises: does this mechanism of social constraint which is opposed to the instinctive drives of the individual explain all cases of guilt feeling or merely some of them?"[2]

Tournier and other Christian psychologists, following Freud's insights into the psychological origins of guilt, began to distinguish between true and false guilt. Tournier indicated, for example, that "the true guilt of men comes from things with which they are reproached by God in their innermost hearts . . . false

1. Paul Tournier, *Guilt and Grace* (New York: Harper, 1961), 63.
2. Ibid., 64.

guilt is that of which comes as a result of the judgments and suggestion of men."[3] In a similar way, Gary Collins, O. Quentin Hyder, and Clyde Maurice Narramore[4] have suggested a distinction between real guilt and false guilt. In a more academic vein, E. Mansell Pattison has distinguished between existential-religious guilt and psychologic guilt.[5] These distinctions are important. They also mark a turning point in the thinking of many Christians regarding guilt, conscience, conviction, and related issues.

The awareness that at least some guilt emotions have their origin in the normal process of personality development is due largely to the influence of psychoanalysis. Probably more than any other person, Freud has made the church stop and think about its concepts of sin and guilt and the consequences of these concepts in the lives of parishioners.

The ramifications of Freud's discovery were tremendous. Christians under the intense burden of guilt could begin to see their way out. Rather than engaging in repeated cycles of confession and self-condemnation they could begin to seek constructive solutions to punitive, neurotic guilt feelings through insight into their dynamic formation. This distinction between real and false guilt also made many ministers and Christian leaders more sensitive to the potential damage done by unnecessarily putting people under a burden of guilt. This is the single most important psychoanalytic contribution to the Christian view of guilt.

The Nature of Guilt Feelings

A second question raised by psychoanalysis is: What exactly is a guilt feeling? Defining these feelings is frequently a problem in discerning a Christian view of guilt. We have not clarified the meaning of the term and, as a result, many parishioners confuse divine conviction with neurotic condemnation. In demon-

3. Ibid., 67.
4. Gary Collins, *Search for Reality* (Wheaton, Ill.: Key, 1969); O. Quentin Hyder, *The Christian's Handbook of Psychiatry* (Fleming, N.J.: Revell, 1971); Clyde Maurice Narramore, *Encyclopedia of Psychological Problems* (Grand Rapids: Zondervan, 1966).
5. E. Mansell Pattison, "On the Failure to Forgive or to Be Forgiven," *American Journal of Psychotherapy* 19 (1965): 106–15.

strating that guilt has specific affective and cognitive components, psychoanalysis puts us in a better position to help the
guilt-ridden person. Freud suggested that guilt was in reality an
internalized fear of punishment and rejection.[6] He also suggested
that a sense of shame and the loss of self-esteem are functions
of superego processes. Although some analytic authors separate
the emotion of shame from the concept of guilt, I prefer to deal
with them together and to conceive of shame as one constituent
element of the guilt emotion.

Seen in this way, guilt is identified as basically an affective
experience comprised of internalized fears of punishment, rejection, and loss of self-esteem. This conceptual understanding of
guilt opens up new doors for biblical applications. Rather than
speaking generally to the emotion of guilt, we can speak specifically to the fear of punishment, the fear of rejection, and the loss
of self-esteem. The biblical doctrine of creation, for example, has
specific implications for self-esteem. Justification by faith speaks
deeply to the fear of punishment. And the concepts of union with
Christ, eternal security, and related doctrines all address the fear
of divine rejection. Rather than try to apply concepts of forgiveness and freedom from guilt in abstract ways, we can move in
with a clear understanding of the painful emotions experienced
by the guilt-ridden person. And with these insights we can apply
the Scripture in an increasingly meaningful way.

The Development of Guilt Feelings

A third question is: Who is responsible for the development of
guilt feelings? I think this is one of the most misunderstood of all
psychoanalytic concepts. The average layperson (and, for that
matter, the average minister) tends to view psychoanalysis as
blaming parents for the development of guilt feelings. Freud did
speak about overly strict superegos, societal standards, and repressed ids. It is easy to gain the impression that Freud encouraged acting out and placed all the blame for guilt emotions on the
parents. Anyone who has read Freud knows, however, that he
made it very clear that the analyst's duty was not to loose an

6. Sigmund Freud, *The Ego and the Id* (New York: W. W. Norton, 1960).

uncontrolled id. Instead he wrote that the task of the analyst was to side with the ego. In a paper entitled "Wild Psychoanalysis," Freud went to some length to make it clear that proper practice of psychoanalysis was not intended to solve neuroses by some form of sexual release or acting out. Freud's concern was not to release the unconscious id impulses but rather to bring the unconscious into consciousness so that it could gradually be brought under the control of the ego.

Who, then, is responsible for the development of guilt feelings? Is it the parents? Or God? Or a psychic process within the individual? Or some combination of these factors?

The view that parents are to blame is one adopted by many psychotherapists (including many "psychoanalytically oriented" therapists who do not fully comprehend the psychoanalytical view of superego development). The view that the Holy Spirit causes guilt feelings is probably the one held by the majority of Christians. I am aware of no one who believes that internal processes alone (apart from either parents or God) account for the development of guilt.

The psychoanalytic view is actually a combination of the above views. Psychoanalysts see guilt feelings as developing both from the inner processes within the individual and from the influence of his or her environment.

Before going into this psychoanalytic view, let me suggest certain limitations of other options. Therapists adhering to the view that guilt feelings come solely from the internalization of parental attitudes (or from conditioned emotional responses) operate on the assumption that guilt-ridden people have lived with guilt-inducing parents. That is, they have had parents who were excessively punitive, who exhibited conditional love, and who frequently attacked or demeaned their children's sense of self-worth or self-esteem. Holding this view of the development of guilt, these therapists see a significant part of their therapeutic task to be to create an accepting atmosphere free of guilt-inducing attitudes. This achievement, combined with insight into the environmental sources of their guilt, is thought to be the essence of the growth process.

This approach can be very helpful, and it is effective as far as it goes. I would suggest, however, that in the light of psychoanalytic thinking this view does not do justice to the development of guilt. The missing element is the role of personal responsibility. Whereas this view makes the guilt-ridden patient a victim of parental hostility, psychoanalysis suggests that the person is also a victim of his or her own hostility.

The concepts of projection and internalization can be used to explain this conclusion. Psychoanalytic theory holds that when infants experience frustration or deprivation, they soon enter a state of rage or anger. At early stages of ego development (when infants still have difficulty clearly distinguishing themselves from their environment) enraged infants see their whole environment as angry. This is the rudimentary experience of projection in which the infant's own emotional experience is put on the entire world.

As infants grow and begin to differentiate themselves from their environment they also become able to transgress certain parental guidelines. Children may see a guideline they do not like, or they feel that their parents do not give them what they want. They become angry and give vent to their frustration by rebelling against the standard. The parents then intervene and discipline. On the basis of the mechanism of internalization children take in their parent's punitive corrective attitudes. These internalized parental punishments, or mental threats, become part of the child's developing superego. They are experienced as guilt, and thereafter the child speaks to himself or herself with the same amount of harshness as the parents did in reality.

At this point one additional factor enters in. Children do not internalize their parents' corrective attitudes as they are in reality. Instead they internalize their parents' attitudes as they perceive them. Their perception has been distorted by their own experience of anger and by the projection of their anger onto the parents. In other words, if children are angry at their parents they naturally expect their parents to harbor a similar amount of anger toward them. Thus when parents respond to children, children perceive the parents' actual anger plus the anger that they impute to them through the mechanism of projection. This tends to exaggerate the degree of punitiveness children see in their parents. It is this projectively distorted image of parents that children internalize into their developing superego. In later life, then, the child's conscience will not be an exact replica of the punitive attitudes of parents. Instead it will reflect an admixture of parental punitiveness plus projected hostility. This means that a person's superego (and consequently his or her guilt feelings) are frequently much more harsh than the parents were in reality. An explanation of adult guilt feelings that places the responsibility entirely on parental corrective attitudes is inadequate.

Therapeutic endeavors that aim only at resolving the effects of parental punitiveness will fall short. While these attitudes must be carefully evaluated and worked through, the core of superego problems will not be resolved until patients come to the understanding that, entirely separate from their parents, they are responsible for some of the punitiveness in their own superego. Even if children had perfect parents, they would still develop some punitive superego attitudes (guilt). The first time they did not get their way they would become angry and would project that anger onto parents. Then they would internalize the parents' attitudes as they perceived them, internalizing their own anger into the superego. In this way psychoanalysis shows how each of us is personally responsible for a good bit of the development of guilt in our own superegos.

The Motivational Effect of Guilt

A fourth contribution that psychoanalysis has made to the Christian view of guilt is to be found in the question, What is the effect of guilt motivation on an individual? In other words, does guilt motivate positive results in the personality, or does it have negative, growth-inhibiting consequences?

While theologians have consistently emphasized a love-motivated biblical morality, unfortunately this emphasis is frequently lost in the pulpit and in the pew. Psychoanalysis reminds us that a morality based on early infantile fears of punishment and abandonment is inadequate as a constructive motivation. This kind of morality spends most of its energy protecting one's own ego rather than focusing on constructive, love-motivated change. In its emphasis on what Pattison has called ego morality, psychoanalysis stresses the importance of moving away from these infantile, superego-centered motivations toward adult, love-motivated moral choices. Pattison comments that morality has been usually thought of in terms of static rules and has been defined as a negative behavior related to avoidance of punitive superego sanctions or meeting ego ideal demands. In contrast, the concept of morality developed here is a dynamic concept emphasizing the selection of goals and values and the process by which the person makes value choices; although including avoidance behavior it emphasizes the positive goal person directed behavior of the ego.[7]

To recast Pattison's point in theological language, we should move from a legalistically based morality toward a love-motivated morality of grace.

The church needs to make a lot of progress in this area. In spite of a wide acceptance of the biblical concepts of grace in theological circles, a large number of Christians sadly lack this experience. Pastors and teachers (and sometimes counselors!) find it more convenient to turn to externally based, legalistically derived, and superego-centered motivations instead of internally based, love-motivated ego choices. This leads to a very shallow view of sin. The typical externals such as murder, theft, sexual sins, and the like still receive much more emphasis in the typical church than do the attitudes of anxiety, depression, anger, jealousy, pride, and so on. If the church could begin to take seriously Freud's concept of the unconscious and the tremendous strength of our repressions we would be in a much better position to apply words of grace exactly where they are needed.

Conclusion

I have elaborated four contributions that psychoanalysis has made and can make to our Christian understanding of the emotion of guilt. I am sure that there are other areas of potential overlap between psychoanalysis and the Christian view of guilt. The whole problem of ambivalence between love and hate in the formation of conscience and the implications of this ambivalence for our desire to be like God and to be his dependent children, has tremendous potential for the integration of biblical and psychoanalytic concepts. We do not have time to delve

7. E. Mansell Pattison, ed., *Clinical Psychiatry and Religion* (Boston: Little, Brown, 1969), 101.

into these issues. I have tried to stimulate thinking about the potential integration of biblical principles with depth-analytical thinking. While no simple marriage of the two perspectives is possible, a deepened understanding of the unconscious and of the many complex dynamics involved in personality development can aid us in applying biblical principles to people in need.

9

Shame and the Human Predicament

BRAD A. BINAU

In a pluralistic world in which God and the church's language about God seem irrelevant to many people, how can we help them grasp the ways in which God is addressing them? That is the underlying concern of this chapter.

Articulating the Word of God through the concepts of law and gospel is one theological approach to the question.[1] According to this view, in God's address to us there is both a "no" and a "yes," and the two are in tension with each other.

The distinction between law and gospel is widely acknowledged in Christian theology. Contemporary theology has explored the meaning of the gospel by pointing to such experiential correlates as forgiveness and acceptance. In pastoral theology, too, the tendency is to discuss the implications of the gospel but not to dwell on the meaning of the law. One looks in vain in recent

---

1. Throughout this chapter I will refer simply to "law" and "gospel," but in each instance it should be understood that we are discussing the *concepts* of law and gospel. Each has a basic referent. Neither can be fully summarized in any one form. The basic referent for the concept of law is death. Whatever confronts us with our limits, including, but not exclusively, the Torah, is law. Conversely, gospel has to do with whatever makes new life possible. Its basic referent is the *kerygma*—that, because of the life, death, and resurrection of Jesus, death is no longer the last word in creation.

pastoral theology texts for a discussion of the Word of God as law
in any experiential or theological depth.[2] We can begin to correct
this omission by considering shame as a possible experiential
correlate to the law. We can accomplish the task by considering
shame from a psychological, biblical, and theological perspective.

The Concept of Law

Law has often been clarified by speaking of its several "uses,"
and it is important to review these at the outset for the sake of our
discussion.

In its civil, or first, use the law of God serves a protective function. It is God speaking a divine "no" to us to curb our sinfulness.
In this sense the command "Do not murder" means "It will be
well for society if human beings do not take one another's lives."

In its didactic, or third, use the law serves a teaching function.
It is a guide to right living in the lives of the regenerate. In this
sense, the imperative "Do not murder" means "This is how children of God should conduct themselves: They should show respect for human life."

The theological, or second, use of the law is the primary focus
of this chapter. This use involves the Word of God as a mirror in
which we see our sinfulness. In this sense the demand "Do not
murder" means "See clearly who you are. You are a person who
must be reminded not to murder because you are filled with desires to dominate your fellow human beings." This divine word
of accusation exposes who we are and drives us to the gospel.
It is the Word of God which "always accuses," which "kills,"
which comes to us as anything that frightens and accuses,
reminding us of our mortality.[3] The law, thus understood, is not a
static concept of *lex aeterna*, the eternal law written on the hearts

2. See William Hulme, *Pastoral Care and Counseling* (Minneapolis: Augsburg, 1981);
William Arnold, *Introduction to Pastoral Care* (Philadelphia: Westminster, 1982); and
Howard Clinebell, *Basic Types of Pastoral Care and Counseling*, 2d ed. (Nashville:
Abingdon, 1984).

3. Philip Melanchthon, "Apology of the Augsburg Confession," *Book of Concord*,
trans. and ed. Theodor G. Tappert (Philadelphia: Fortress, 1959), 112; Martin Luther,
"Answer to the Hyperchristian, Hyperspiritual, and Hyperlearned Book by Goat
Emserin Leipzig," *Luther's Works* (Philadelphia: Fortress, 1963), 183; Gerhard Forde,
The Law-Gospel Debate (Minneapolis: Augsburg, 1969), 177.

of men and women to instruct. Instead it is dynamic in character, a characteristic Rodney Hunter clarifies when he notes that, "The law, understood in its full significance, is much more like a force or an event or an agency than a mere codex in the Latin sense of *lex*. It is not that the so-called content of the Law is unimportant theologically, but that its specific content is of secondary significance to its dynamic reality as a spiritual force or event."[4]

I believe that when the law of God addresses us in this way it defines the predicament to which the gospel responds. I also believe that we must have a clear and proper understanding of our predicament before we can grasp the meaning of our salvation.

A Psychological Understanding of Shame and Guilt

Traditionally, the law of God has been linked to the *feeling* of guilt. Being addressed by the law makes us aware of our guilt. This correlation between law and guilt has merit, but is not exhaustive. In fact, our understanding of the law deepens as we begin to develop an appreciation for the dynamics of shame, especially since we know much more about shame today than we did even ten years ago. We know that guilt and shame, while related, have different causes and give rise to different defenses. Distinguishing between the two can help us to articulate the human predicament and to know how the Word of God addresses us.

Shame and guilt can be distinguished as transgression versus failure. At the core, guilt suggests that we have *gone beyond what was allowed* while shame points to the fact that we have *fallen short of what was expected*. We can illustrate the difference with two case studies; a third shows how the difference is often confused.

Arthur Becker, in *Guilt: Curse or Blessing*, reports the following words of an unnamed woman:

> My husband walked out on me tonight. I know he isn't going to come back. It's my fault too. The whole thing is my fault. This isn't the first time this has happened. But I am sure he means it. The

4. Rodney Hunter, "Law and Gospel in Pastoral Care," *Journal of Pastoral Care* 30 (Sept. 1976): 154.

broken door, well, I did that. I told him that he didn't need to come back and then I slammed the door. It's my temper. I get so mad at him that I lose my mind and don't know what I'm doing. It is always my fault. If I could just control my temper. I have tried about everything. I've prayed about it but it just doesn't seem to do any good. Tonight he just left for good.[5]

The woman's language reveals a sense of transgression. She is concerned, not about adequacy, but about actions. Her temper has been excessive and has precipitated behavior that went beyond the bounds of civility, as the broken door indicates. Especially noteworthy is the woman's lack of denial. Her feelings are not masked with rage, as is often the case with shame. Absent too is the sense of confusion that usually characterizes shame. She has no difficulty in stating clearly, "It is my fault." She is aware of, and feels responsible for, what she has done. The situation of Mrs. A. is quite different:

At age sixty-eight, Mrs. A was dying of cancer. A faithful church member, we can presume she had a good relationship with her own pastor. Nonetheless, she requested a visit from her son's pastor in order to relate a painful incident from her past. For almost twenty years she had been president of her women's group but was burdened by how she had conducted herself in that role on a particular occasion. "Once," she relates, "when the girls were going to consider another president, I—I did a terrible thing. I let them think the other woman was . . . not good enough." The pastor responds that we are "bound to fail once in a while"—an understatement to be sure, but true nevertheless! Then, by way of theological interpretation, the pastor comments that God's forgiveness is available for such failures. With a tired expression Mrs. A. responds, "I suppose forgiveness is ours."[6]

What can account for Mrs. A's unenthusiastic response to the pastor's reassurance? I think she remains unmoved, because the pastor has misdiagnosed the situation. Associating failure with guilt, he offers forgiveness as the cure. However, failure—the ex-

5. This case is discussed by Arthur Becker in *Guilt: Curse or Blessing?*, (Minneapolis: Augsburg, 1977), 5–6.
6. This case, analyzed in Donald Capps, *Life Cycle Theory and Pastoral Care* (Philadelphia: Fortress, 1983), was originally presented in *Casebook in Pastoral Counseling*, eds. Newman S. Cryer, Jr., and John M. Vayhinger (Nashville: Abingdon, 1962), 267–70.

perience of falling short of what was expected—is more a matter of shame. It is true that Mrs. A has in some sense "transgressed." She bore false witness against her neighbor, and it is good to remind ourselves that shame and guilt can never be separated completely. Yet Mrs. A is troubled less by her transgression (an excessive use of power) than she is by the insufficient amount of self-control that she displayed in allowing others to think ill of her competitor. The realization that she has been less than what she and others expected has produced shame. Her shame requires a different response than does guilt. It requires, not an assurance of forgiveness, but a word of acceptance in spite of her failures.

A final vignette illustrates the tendency to confuse shame and guilt.

> Richard, a salesman in his early 60's, recently sat in my study and talked about his marital difficulties. The marriage was not yet over, but it was clearly headed in that direction and Richard was in obvious pain. His wife of some thirty years had declined to relocate with him when his company transferred him to our part of the country. He had hoped the separation would be only temporary, but as each day passed it was clearer to him that it would likely become permanent. "Pastor," he said, "I just don't understand it. In all our years of marriage I never once cheated on my wife. I never drank. I don't smoke. I just wish she would tell me what I did, then I could fix things."

Richard was struggling to articulate his problem in terms of guilt. He felt pain and assumed that it was related to some transgression that he had committed. As he saw it, if he could only rectify his wrongdoing the pain would subside and his wife would return. Richard's question, "What did I do?" puts the emphasis on his actions. Yet, it would appear that he has *done* nothing wrong. At the heart of his pain is a feeling of failure for not being all that his wife wanted. Thus while he struggled to understand his situation in terms of the more familiar emotion of guilt, it seems that his experience would be described more accurately as one of shame.

One of the things that shame and guilt have in common is that they both arise from tension, though the sources of the tension are different. In classic psychoanalytic terms, the tension that gives rise to guilt is between the ego and the superego while the tension giving rise to shame is between the ego and the ego ideal.[7] This means that when we experience a contradiction between who we *are* (ego) and what we should *do* (superego), we experience guilt. When we experience a contradiction between who we *are* (ego) and what we *want to be* (ego ideal), we experience shame. The distinction, then, is along the lines of doing and being, with guilt focusing on actions and shame focusing on identity.

When guilt occurs it appears that one's sense of self is more stable, more intact than it is in shame. "I may do some bad things, but basically I am okay," is the internal dialogue of the person wrestling with guilt. The woman with an excessive temper in our first case study is an illustration of this dialogue. And Richard, who could see nothing amiss in who he was, could only contemplate what wrongful actions he may have perpetrated. In situations of shame, the ego is under siege from comparisons with a more perfect, that is, a more whole, ego ideal. "I may occasionally do some good things, but basically I am not okay," is the internal dialogue of the person wrestling with shame. Mrs. A seems closer to this disposition.

Shame and guilt also imply different threats. The threat implied by guilt, according to Gerhard Piers, is mutilation. If we transgress, literally "step beyond," we incur the risk of being "cut back." From this view the relationship of guilt to castration anxiety makes perfect sense. Shame, on the other hand, implies abandonment. When it surfaces within our inadequacy and sense of failure, we incur the threat of being "cut off." Piers has referred to this as "death by emotional starvation."[8]

A final distinction between shame and guilt is that shame tends to occur within relationships in a way that guilt does not. In large part this is because our capacity for shame develops prior to our capacity for guilt, during the stage when the question of who we are in relationships is first being addressed.

Erik Erikson's epigenetic theory of human development is significant in this regard. Erikson argues that the initial task of a human being is to develop the confidence that relationships are possible, the relationship with the mother being the primary example. This confidence needs to develop during the first months

7. See Gerhard Piers and Milton B. Singer, *Shame and Guilt* (New York: W. W. Norton, 1971).

8. Ibid., 29.

of life, during the stage that Erikson labels "trust versus mistrust." The acquisition of this confidence makes possible the move toward autonomy in the second stage.

Paradoxically, Erikson suggests that we become autonomous through relatedness. In other words, we do not develop in a vacuum. To become an individual, we need to take a decisive step in the direction of another person. Shame is always a possibility in this context. It is a feeling that we do not "measure up" against those persons in whom we have some relational investment. It does not represent a break in the relational bond, but in fact is often accompanied by an intense desire to repair the damaged relationship. As Carl Schneider observes, "In shame, the object one is alienated from, one also loves still."[9] The following vignette illustrates the point.

> A twelve-year-old boy has begun to value his relationship with a considerably older brother, even desiring to emulate him. The two make plans to purchase season football tickets, an activity highly prized by the older, for the coming year. This is in the fall and all throughout that next year the young boy expectantly looks ahead to the exciting adventure with his older brother. Little need be said of the forthcoming event, yet the boy has come to count on it. That spring, the older brother becomes engaged and marries later that summer. In the fall, with football season approaching, nothing more is said of their prior plan to go to the games. In fact, the brother and his new wife purchase the coveted football tickets for themselves, with not a word being said to the young boy. The boy's expectations are smashed, suddenly exposed as wrong. The very thing he has come silently to depend upon is exposed as inconsequential to the *deeply valued older brother*. [emphasis author's][10]

This twelve-year-old is experiencing shame. He suspects that there is something wrong with him, even as he continues to value his older brother.

Recalling that the implied fear associated with guilt is punishment, as opposed to the fear of abandonment that is associated with shame, we can see that guilt focuses our concern on what will happen to *me*. Shame, on the other hand, focuses on the ques-

9. Carl Schneider, *Shame, Exposure, and Privacy* (Boston: Beacon Hill, 1977), 28.
10. Gershen Kaufman, *Shame: The Power of Caring* (Cambridge, Mass.: Shenkman, 1980), 15–16.

tion, "What will happen to this relationship, a relationship that means so much to me?" Later, we will return to this topic and will consider the theological significance of shame and damaged relationships, especially our damaged relationship to God. In the meantime, we can sharpen our understanding of shame by shifting our focus from a psychological perspective to a biblical perspective.

A Biblical Understanding of Shame

The words *shame* and *ashamed* occur more frequently in the Old Testament than in the New by a ratio of better than four to one. That does not mean, however, that shame is less important in the New Testament.

The New Testament

New Testament references to shame are made almost entirely in terms of the Greek word *aischunō* and its cognates.[11] This word is used most frequently in the Septuagint to render the Hebrew *bôš* and *bôšet*, the most common Hebrew terms conveying the idea of shame. Rudolf Bultmann finds *aischunō* usually means "to bring to shame," and he notes that God is the subject, the one who shames. "The shame . . . he brings is his judgment."[12]

Kee concurs, noting that the primary reference in the Septuagint when *aischunō* is used is not to a feeling of shame but to an act of divine judgment.[13] Kee's essay is part of a larger attempt to interpret the thought of Mark. He focuses on Mark 8:38. This verse highlights the primary issue that Kee believes to be at stake regarding the biblical use of "shame," whether it be in the Jesus tradition (of which Mark 8:38 is a part) or in the other Old or New Testament references. The primary theme is eschatological vindication/judgment based on the nature of the relationship between believers and their Creator. The "experience of shame is the des-

11. According to Howard Clark Kee, there is no significant difference between the root *aischunō* and its derivatives *epaischunō* and *kataischunō*. Howard Clark Kee, "The Linguistic Background of 'Shame' in the New Testament," *On Language, Culture, and Religion*, ed. Matthew Black (The Hague, Netherlands: Mouton, 1974), 134.

12. Rudolf Bultmann, "αισχύνω," *Theological Dictionary of the New Testament*, 4 vols., ed. Gerhard Kittel and trans. Geoffrey Bromiley (Grand Rapids: Eerdmans, 1964), 1: 189–91.

13. Kee, *Linguistic Background of "Shame,"* 134.

tiny of the enemies," while "deliverance from shame is the vindi-cation of the faithful."[14] Kee clarifies the issue by paraphrasing Mark 8:38:

> Whoever becomes disillusioned with Jesus and his words or de-fects from them by reason of persecution or the rigor of the de-mands of discipleship will find himself "put to shame" under divine judgment through the agency of the eschatological judge, the Son of Man, in the end time.[15]

Kee's interpretation of this passage is that "those who have lost or who never had confidence in Jesus as God's agent for bringing in the New Age will be 'put to shame' in the day of eschatological judgment."[16] It is true that only the negative side of the vindica-tion/judgment issue is present explicitly in this Marcan passage. Kee argues, however, that the positive side is implied and is more explicit in a passage such as Jeremiah 17:18: "Let those be put to shame who persecute me, but let me not be put to shame; Let them be dismayed, but let me not be destroyed."[17]

Two important points surface from these New Testament re-flections. First, there is a relational aspect to the word *shame* as it is used in the Bible. People who are in a trusting relationship with God experience vindication while those who are not experience judgment. Second, there is a close link between shame and the theme of judgment, which seems to corroborate our assertion that shame is a manifestation of the law. To experience God's judgment is to be convicted by the Word of God as law, indicating that one is not in a right relationship with the Creator and the rest of creation because of misplaced trust.

The Old Testament

The Old Testament has more words to express the experience of shame than does the New Testament[18] and yet there is a sur-prising consistency in the meaning of shame throughout the Old

14. Ibid., 141.
15. Ibid., 146.
16. Ibid.
17. Ibid.
18. For instance, while *aischunō* and its cognates constitute nearly all New Testament Greek references to shame, in the Hebrew Old Testament *bôš, bôšet, ḥŏpăr, yābăš, kŏlăm, kĕlimŏh,* and *gŏlŏh* are used.

Testament. Most of the time the notions of being "confounded" or "confused" are associated with shame. In fact, some of the same words translated as "shame" are translated as "confounded,"[19] at least in the King James Version.

If we understand the basic meaning of "confuse" and "confound," we know that at times they are the preferred translation and can help us to understand the biblical conception of shame. "Confuse" and "confound" come from the same Latin root, *confundere*, meaning essentially "to pour, or mix, together." The *Oxford Latin Dictionary*[20] indicates a broader range of meaning for the term. One can detect, in fact, movement from something specific (as in "to mix together") to something considerably less well-defined (as in alternative meanings, such as "to disorder, upset, destroy"). It is this broader, more dire experience that comes through in the English word *confound*, especially when the *Oxford English Dictionary*[21] offers meanings such as "to defeat utterly, bring to nought, overthrow." One meaning specifically links "confound" with "to put to shame, ashamed." The English word *confuse*, coming from the same Latin root as "confound," is also linked with shame.

All of this is to say that shame, as it is reflected in what it means to be "confused" or "confounded," describes a dire predicament, especially in the Old Testament. To be ashamed or confounded (Heb. *bôš*) is to be more than simply "disappointed," as some translations render Psalm 22:5. It means a lack of clarity and definition about one's existence which proves in the end to be one's undoing. Thus to be "confounded" is to be "exposed" or "disoriented," as Donald Capps has described shame.[22]

Fear of exposure and hope of deliverance are important themes in the psalms. "I cleave to thy testimonies, O Lord; let me not be put to shame" (Ps. 119:31 KJV; cf. Ps. 25:2–3a). Shame is the deserved fate of those who do not trust God. The whole of Psalm 83 is a prayer for shame to engulf the enemies of Israel (cf. Ps. 25:3b).

Shame is the experience of having our misplaced trust exposed. It is the realization that our confidence was placed in con-

---

19. *Bôš* is the most frequent example in this regard, though *ḥŏpăr*, *yābăš*, and *kŏlăm* are also translated as "confounded."

20. "Confundō," *Oxford Latin Dictionary* (Oxford, England: Clarendon, 1968), 1: 403.

21. "Confound," *Oxford English Dictionary* (New York: Macmillan, 1888), 2: 813.

22. Capps, *Life Cycle Theory*, 81.

ditional promises and that we are brought up short, resulting in confusion and disorientation. People often describe moments of intense shame with the words, "I wanted to die," as if to say that shame is so painfully confusing to one's existence that nonexistence would be preferable. Carl Schneider, in *Shame, Exposure, and Privacy,*[23] cites instances of people making such remarks in therapy. His observation underscores the relationship between shame and the concept of law, which has death as its referent. Paul Pruyser suggests that Nathan's confrontation with David be interpreted along the same lines (2 Sam. 12). According to Pruyser, the prophet's words, "You are the man," evoked deep shame in David. Characteristically, this shame points inexorably toward death, and though David himself was spared, the story accounts for this fact through the death of his infant son.[24]

An examination of Isaiah's "Third Servant Song" illustrates how the Bible understands the human predicament in terms of shame, as well as how shame (or law) is not necessarily God's last word. In Isaiah 50:7 the servant says: "For the LORD helps me; therefore I have not been confounded; therefore I have set my face like a flint and I know that I shall not be put to shame" (KJV).

This passage indicates that the one who is in a trusting relationship with God is helped and will not be destroyed by those who work contrary to the divine will. By implication, it is the one out of relationship with God who suffers these distresses. It is true that the faithful servant, according to the preceding verse, has suffered.[25] Still, verse 7 would seem to indicate that through the strength of the relationship with God, the injuries suffered by the servant will not be the servant's undoing. All of this becomes clearer in chapter 54 when God responds to the servant. The plight of the servant has changed: God is the reason for the change.[26] "You will not be ashamed," "You will not be put to shame," "You will forget the shame of your youth," is God's assurance to Israel (Isa. 54:4 RSV). The suffering of past shame (or law) is alleviated by the formulation of a new covenant.

23. Schneider, *Shame, Exposure*, 78–79.
24. Paul Pruyser, "Nathan and David: A Psychological Footnote," *Pastoral Psychology* 13 (Feb. 1962): 14–18.
25. Claus Westermann, *Isaiah 40–46: A Commentary* (Philadelphia: Westminster, 1969), 230–31.
26. Ibid., 271.

These Old Testament reflections in general, and Isaiah 50:7 in particular, open up new ways of understanding a basic tenet of evangelical theology—the doctrine of salvation by grace through faith. Salvation (from death which confronts us as law or shame) is by grace (the divinely given possibility of relationship) through faith (the redirection of our trust from conditional to unconditional promises).

A Theological Understanding of Shame

We have seen that there is a relational aspect to shame in the Bible, primarily because the biblical view of human existence is a relational one. This relational anthropology is centered in the notion of covenant.

Covenant, according to Walter Brueggemann, is a way of perceiving reality. Its claim is that human persons are grounded in Another who initiates personhood and who stays bound to persons in loyal ways for their well-being. Brueggemann characterizes God's covenanting action under four headings.

1. God alone creates new things from old (*creatio ex nihilo*).
2. God does this through speech, through the Word.
3. Covenanting establishes a divine/human relationship that is antithetical to notions of human autonomy.
4. By covenanting with us God redefines human life.[27]

Experiences of shame draw painful attention to the fact that this sense of covenant has been violated and that our lives are relationally askew. They illumine our understanding of the human predicament and our need for the gospel. Our predicament is not simply that we are bad or wrong. Rather our wrongness has a context—a relational context. In a basic way, then, the human predicament has to do with estrangement in relationships, and it is this very fact that shame exposes.

Exposure is a basic characteristic of the nature of shame.[28] The word comes from the Latin *exponere*, "to put out," or "to place

27. Walter Brueggemann, "Covenanting as Human Vocation," *Interpretation* 33 (April 1979): 115–29.
28. Helen Merrell Lynd, *On Shame and the Search for Identity* (New York: Harcourt, Brace, 1958), 27–34.

out," or, as Carl Schneider notes, "shame arises when something doesn't fit." "Thus we experience shame when we feel we are placed out of the context within which we wish to be interpreted. Shame occasions are those when someone or some aspect of a person or group is 'out of place,' that is, is exposed."[29]

At the heart of this "out-of-placeness" is the "disunion" that Dietrich Bonhoeffer connects with shame. If we are in right relationship with God and others, the pain of exposure would not exist. Instead we would experience it as illumination or useful insight. But given our situation, the "flooding searchlight of shame," as Ernest Kurtz describes it, acts not so much as "a lamp to our feet and a light to our path" (Ps. 119:105) than as a surgical laser beam that lays bare the root cause of our predicament.

A brief digression is in order. The theological perspective on shame that we have developed has important implications for therapy. We must be attentive to the dangers of shame that may operate in a therapeutic strategy that relies heavily on insight. Because of the reality of the law in human experience, insight about oneself can be experienced as shameful exposure. Unless we are prepared and equipped to deal with this pain, the experience is likely to provoke the counselee's defenses and drive him or her even farther into hiding. One way to keep this from happening in therapy is to balance the need for self-discovery with the need to maintain an "interpersonal bridge" of relationships.

We have already noted that shame and law have in common the characteristic of exposure. Where the law is concerned it is sin that is exposed—the sin of misplaced trust. Luther explains that the law's second use, its chief function or power,

> is to make original sin manifest and show man to what utter depths his nature has fallen and how corrupt it has become. So the law must tell him that he neither has nor cares for God or that he worships strange gods—something that he would not have believed before without a knowledge of the law. Thus he is terror-striken and humbled, becomes despondent and despairing, anxiously desires help but does not know where to find it, and begins to be alienated from God.[30]

29. Schneider, *Shame, Exposure*, 35.
30. "Smalcald Articles," art. 2, pt. 3, Tappert, trans., *Book of Concord*, 303.

Does shame also expose sin? Yes, especially if we take a view of sin that is consistent with the relational anthropology and the constructive theology that we have presented. Bonhoeffer, who is one of the few theologians who has dealt with shame, maintains that "shame is man's ineffaceable recollection of his estrangement from the origin; it is grief for this estrangement, and the powerless longing to return to unity with the origin."[31] Thus both shame as Bonhoeffer suggests and law as Luther suggests point to the fact that our covenantal relationship with God has been broken.

Paul Tillich contrasts "sin" with "sins," citing the former as a description of the overall human predicament and the latter as trespasses against a list of rules (albeit a divinely given list).[32] I am not convinced that we can draw the line between the two as neatly as Tillich would like, but when we seek to discover the nature of the sin that the law and shame expose, Tillich is helpful. He identifies "sin" with estrangement, with "our act of turning away from participation in the divine Ground from which we come and to which we go."[33] It is "the disruption of an essential unity" and reflects alienation not only from God and others but also from oneself.[34]

Bonhoeffer's insightful comments about shame and disunion are appropriate to this part of the discussion as well. His anthropology and his understanding of sin are quite similar to Tillich's. He describes the predicament of a human being as "disunion with God, with men, with things, and with himself."[35] Shame arises as this disunion comes to consciousness.

The overcoming of shame and the silencing of the voice of the law depend entirely on the healing of the estrangement that is the human condition. The very notions of estrangement and alienation elicit the image of a split or a tear, a "disunion," that must be mended. This is yet another reason why the image of sin as es-

31. Dietrich Bonhoeffer, *Ethics*, trans. Neville H. Smith, ed. Eberhard Bethge (New York: Macmillan, 1955), 23.

32. Paul Tillich, *Systematic Theology*, 3 vols. (Chicago: University of Chicago Press, 1951–1963), 2: 46.

33. Paul Tillich, *The Eternal Now* (New York: Charles Scribner's Sons, 1963), 56.

34. Paul Tillich, "Estrangement and Reconciliation," *Review of Religion* 9 (Nov. 1944): 6. Tillich's observation that sin involves turning away from the divine Ground is reflected in my thesis that, at a basic level, sin is related more to mistrust than to misdeeds.

35. Bonhoeffer, *Ethics*, 20.

trangement is so powerful, because it correlates so well with reconciliation of salvation (which comes from the Latin root *salvus*,
meaning "health" and "wholeness"). "Shame can be overcome
only when the original unity is restored, when man is once again
clothed by God in the other man, in the 'house which is from
Heaven,' the Temple of God (2 Cor. 5:2ff)."[36]

Baptism as a Pastoral Resource for Shame

Our primary pastoral task concerning persons suffering from
shame is to assist them to return from isolation to relationship.
Because it is an experiential correlate of law and because, like
law, shame has death as a referent, it exposes us and "puts us out"
of relationship. Like death, it points toward the end of our humanity when it threatens relationships, since it is only in and through
relationships that we become fully human.

How are we to assist this return to relationship? Gershen Kaufman, in *Shame: The Power of Caring*, makes many useful suggestions.[37] John Patton in *Is Human Forgiveness Possible?* is also
helpful.[38] In both cases the authors focus on what can be done
therapeutically. Their comments, while insightful, deserve to be
enhanced theologically.

I believe that baptismal theology, as well as the sacrament of
baptism itself, are great assets in encouraging people to return to
relationship. This proposal may not make immediate sense to
many readers. If so, I suspect that the pastoral and theological
significance of baptism for shame is not immediately apparent,
because we frequently operate with a pre-Reformation baptismal
theology that is based on a guilt paradigm for the human predicament.

The sacramental system devised by scholasticism (the theology
of the pre-Reformation church) seemingly provided an answer for
every problem that sinful human nature presented. In this sense
it was an ingenious pastoral tool. Its effectiveness rested on the
fact that the system not only provided answers but that it also
dictated the framework within which the human predicament
could be conceived. The human "problem," according to this pre-

---

36. Ibid., 23.
37. Kaufman, *Shame*, see especially chap. 5.
38. John Patton, *Is Human Forgiveness Possible?* (Nashville: Abingdon, 1985), 180–82.

Reformation view, was with concupiscence. Strictly speaking, concupiscence was not equated with sin, but it was described as a human being's inherited inclination to sin. Baptism worked a change on the person's concupiscent nature. Concupiscence was weakened or truncated, although a kind of "tinder" (*fomes peccati*) remained that could easily be fanned into the flames of sin by temptation. Grace imparted through the other sacraments gave a person power over such temptation.

In this system, baptism effected a change of character, making it less likely that the individual would fall into sin. The ground on which this system rested was a "guilt paradigm." Transgressions were the problem, so lessening one's capacity to transgress, or at least providing ways to make amends for transgressions, became the solution. To the extent that we still understand baptism primarily as the irradication of original sin, to that extent we continue to think of baptism from the perspective of a guilt paradigm.

It was Martin Luther who grasped the fact that a person can be a sinner and at the same time justified. Consequently, the focus of his baptismal theology—a focus that continues to challenge our theological and anthropological assumptions—shifted from the nature of a person's character to the nature of the relationship between a person and God. This shift was made possible by the realization that the righteousness of God is not "active" but "passive." That is to say, God's righteousness is not associated with wrath but with grace. God's passive righteousness was for Luther a description of our personal relationship with God.[39] *Deus pro nobis*—"God for us"—became central to Luther's baptismal thinking.

The consequence of Luther's insight was that baptism was taken out of a context in which it related to misdeeds and was redefined and related primarily to mistrust. Through its unconditional promise of acceptance, making us members of the body of Christ and full heirs in the family of God (Gal. 3:27–29; 1 Cor. 12:13; Rom. 8:15–17), baptism stands as a daily invitation to re-evaluate what we trust to give meaning to our lives. Since shame

39. Cf. Martin Brecht, *Martin Luther: His Road to Reformation. 1483–1521.* trans. James L. Schaaf (Philadelphia: Fortress, 1985), 226; Martin Luther, "The Argument of St. Paul's Epistle to the Galatians," *Luther's Works*, vol. 26 (St. Louis: Concordia, 1963).

arises when we place our unconditional trust in conditional promises, its painful effects can begin to be reversed as our trust is redirected to the kinds of promises offered in baptism, to those that are not conditioned by death.

Finally, of course, we cannot push people into the relationships needed to overcome shame. People must decide for themselves whether they are ready to risk the possibility of shame in a future relationship in order to have the opportunity to participate in the healing that such a relationship can bring. What we can do as pastors and theologians is to clear away some of the obstacles that may hinder people from taking such a step. We can help people focus more intently on the role that promises play in their lives. We can help them to discover the promises that they are trusting and can help them to articulate the pain that comes when this trust is betrayed. More positively, we can present baptism—in our preaching, our teaching, and in our personal relating—as a promise that God will not forsake us. In this way, we can point people to the trustworthy promises of the gospel and invite them to seek enduring meaning by trusting these promises above all others.

10

Pastoral Counseling and Self-Justification

LeRoy Aden

People have an intense longing to be made right. They may want to get right with themselves, with others, and/or with God. They feel, however vaguely, that there is something wrong with them, and they desire, however fervently, to become acceptable.

Christian theology maintains that people try to become right through their own efforts, through what Paul calls the law and Martin Luther calls good works. Both men have something very positive and noble in mind. They refer to a life that seeks to obey God's moral and ritual commands. They know that the attempt to fulfill the law is in itself suspect because it is an egoistic attempt to be the source of one's own righteousness, but when they refer to the doing of the law they have in mind the performance of something positive and praiseworthy—the attempt to live an honorable and blameless life.

Pastoral care and counseling indicate that the attempt to make oneself right is more involved and complex. It is not exhausted by the positive attempt to fulfill the law, though that is always an important aspect of self-justification. Actually, it is often a negative and destructive endeavor, one that is more gruesome than either Paul or Luther would have us believe. We can use the data of pastoral counseling to uncover its concrete destructiveness. We find that the whole process can be broken down into three component endeavors, into what I will call a life of suffering, a life of contrived virtue, and a life of insatiable demands. Each endeavor permeates the totality of an individual's life and contributes a unique flavor to the individual's feverish attempt to become right by his or her own efforts.

A Life of Suffering

Mrs. Demand, a thirty-five-year-old woman who became pregnant out of wedlock in her late teens, terminated the pregnancy by a self-induced abortion. She emerged with a nagging sense of guilt and spent years trying to make herself right with God through various schemes of suffering. "When I had all my kids, I asked God to make it terrible for me. 'Pay me back. Make me suffer. Go ahead.' But nothing ever happened." What Mrs. Demand was not aware of was the extent to which the need to suffer had become a dominant part of her life. The "good self" carried on a constant war against the "bad self," seeking to punish, even to destroy, the bad self for its violation of what ought to be. In this respect, Mrs. Demand illustrates one of Sigmund Freud's astute observations: "Our patients do not believe us when we ascribe an 'unconscious sense of guilt' to them; in order to become even moderately intelligible to them we have to explain that the sense of guilt expresses itself in an unconscious seeking for punishment."[1]

As Mrs. Demand became aware of her need to be punished, she also got a glimpse of its intensity and depth. It threatened to carry her to the brink of self-destruction, either by a slow, tortuous process of self-negation or by a single dramatic swerve into the path of on-coming cars. "It's like I'm on a collision course, and I can't do anything about it. I work at home until I collapse. And when I drive down the parkway, I have to watch myself or I'll weave into the other lane."

Freud offered a psychological explanation for this kind of be-

---

1. Sigmund Freud, *Civilization and Its Discontents*, trans. Joan Riviere (New York: Doubleday, 1958), 91.

havior. He believed that aggression is an innate part of a person and that therefore it can be modified but never totally eliminated from the individual's psychic economy. The individual, then, has only two real choices: to turn the aggression inward against the self or to turn it outward toward others. Since the latter choice goes against the intent of society to bind individuals together into a cohesive whole, society stands against the expression of aggression and seeks to hold it in check by sending it back to the individual. Thus the individual's aggressiveness is internalized and is taken over by the moral arm of the personality, the superego. The superego, in turn, becomes unduly harsh and directs its hostile demands against the ego. Laboring under these demands, the ego begins to accept, even to seek after, a punitive and self-negating style of life.

The whole process sets up a vicious cycle. Freud describes it succinctly by saying that the superego becomes sadistic and the ego masochistic. On the one hand, the individual possesses an overdemanding conscience which threatens punishment for the slightest offense, and, on the other hand, he or she is tormented by guilt and has an unconscious need to suffer and be punished. Freud believed that this whole process is often unknown to the individual who manifests it. Consequently, it can operate in a vicious and subtle way, for example, as an intense but puzzling resistance to cure. If patients have a strong need to be punished, they may resist the help of therapy in order to protect the suffering and the punishment that is bound up with their illness.

Freud's psychological explanation of why guilty persons are so punitive toward themselves is suggestive. On a theoretical level it relates their harsh sense of guilt to a basic event in their characterological development; on a clinical level it highlights some of the psychological dynamics that are operative when an individual welcomes or even pursues a life of suffering.

Without trying to minimize the importance of Freud's contribution, I think the situation can be viewed from a different angle, one that is suggestive on a clinical and a theological level. Mrs. Demand alludes to it when she says in despair: "I can't go on this way. I can't hate myself more than I already do. I can't torture myself anymore. And all this frantic searching and trying does not help one bit."

Mrs. Demand implies that she is suffering and destroying herself in order to try to make herself acceptable. In other words, punishment for her is an act of purgation, a way of life in which she is paying an indeterminate price for wrongdoing in order to become released from its condemnation. Freud considers this possibility when he tries to explain resistance to cure: "In the end we come to see that we are dealing with what may be called a 'moral' factor; a sense of guilt, which is finding atonement in the illness and is refusing to give up the penalty of suffering."[2] Because Freud never develops this point, he fails to pursue what in my experience as a pastoral counselor is a frequent and decisive purpose of suffering. Individuals who feel unacceptable take matters into their own hands and try to work themselves out of it, either in a relative way by living a life of critical self-doubt or in an ultimate way by living a life of destructive self-sacrifice. They may even proceed on the primitive assumption that in degree, if not in kind, the punishment should fit the crime, so that their whole life may represent a drastic and costly payment. Mrs. Demand manifests this tendency when she implies that, just as guilt came by taking the life of an unborn child, so release must come by taking her own.

If Mrs. Demand illustrates the cost of trying to justify oneself through a life of suffering, she also points to its futility. "All this frantic searching and trying does not help one bit." Suffering, no matter how much, always leaves unanswered the question, "How much is enough?" Furthermore, suffering, no matter how drastic, is always ambiguous, always a mixture of willingness and resentment. Individuals may feel compelled to suffer, but they seldom do it with their whole heart. Consequently, suffering becomes an occasion of further guilt, and not just an unadulterated act of meritorious payment. Individuals may climb on the altar of suffering, or even on the altar of self-destruction, but in the end they rise above the ashes to confront the ambiguity of their sacrifice. In this confrontation they know that their unacceptable state has increased as much as it has been cancelled.

2. Sigmund Freud, *The Ego and the Id*, trans. Joan Riviere (London: Hogarth, 1950), 71.

A Life of Contrived Virtue

To make themselves acceptable unacceptable persons must wage a more positive war than simply a war of suffering. Consequently, they often become entangled in what can be called a life of contrived virtue, that is, a pervasive attempt to make themselves appear better than they really are. On an obvious level they pursue this goal through a life of good works, but counseling also indicates that they pursue it in a subtle and more intangible way. This involves the individual's relation with himself or herself and results in a radical split between what is acceptable and what is unacceptable. Psychologically, we are talking about the process of repression.

"The essence of repression lies simply in the function of rejecting and keeping something out of consciousness."[3] In other words, repression is disowning unacceptable parts of one's life. It can be used against guilt, especially since guilt is a unitary phenomenon that has both an objective and a subjective side. Objectively, it refers to the condition of the individual's life relative to some norm or expectation; subjectively, it refers to the individual's awareness of his or her condition. In other words, guilt is both a fact and a feeling, something we are and something we experience. Normally, there should be a one-to-one correspondence between these two, but unfortunately individuals can, and often do, introduce a split between them. They interject an egocentric desire between what they are guilty of and what they feel guilty for, so the latter conforms more to what they want to feel guilty for rather than to what they are actually guilty of. The purpose of this maneuver is obviously defensive, that is, individuals use their capacity for limited self-determination to avoid real guilt by feeling remorse for a less traumatic and incriminating guilt. In this way they cover up the depth of their guilt and make themselves appear better and more acceptable than they really are.

Sigmund Freud did not develop this understanding of repression. His approach was more psychological than moral, revolving around the heuristic idea that the repression of guilt does not nullify its existence or rob it of its power. Guilt continues to exist

3. Sigmund Freud, "Repression," ed. Ernest Jones, *Collected Papers* (London: Hogarth and the Institute of Psycho-Analysis, 1956), 4: 86.

behind the mask of conscious awareness and exerts a significant influence on the individual's present perception and behavior. Specifically, it can distort the person's contemporary sense of guilt. It causes him or her to read into the current situation a culpability that was actually incurred at an earlier time. As long as individuals remain unaware of the real source of their guilt, they are not able to resolve it properly or to prevent its reappearance in the next situation. Thus their last state is worse than the first. Instead of being released from guilt, repression has embroiled them in an enslaving and anachronistic battle with it.

In addition to this psychological understanding of repression, I am convinced that repression must also be seen as a tool of self-justification. Guilty persons, whether aware of their guilt or not, try to present a facade of goodness. They use repression to create a life of contrived virtue. This tendency is epitomized in persons whose whole life revolves around the attempt to establish their innocence and self-righteousness. They are Dietrich Bonhoeffer's "Pharisee"[4] insofar as they are persons "to whom only the knowledge of good and evil has come to be of importance" in their entire life. They are individuals who, in the face of feeling unrighteous, are driven to establish an outer coating of goodness and virtue as a way to try to make themselves more acceptable.

Actually, a life of contrived virtue is a pseudo-fulfillment of the law. For Judaism, fulfillment of the law means in a minimum sense the doing of the letter of the law and in a maximum sense obedience to the spirit of the law. Contrived virtue is neither of these. It is not interested in doing what is pleasing to God but is concerned to present a fabricated goodness in the hope that it will be acceptable to God. By the same token, it does not represent an obedience of the heart but instead is a facade of acceptability according to one's own rules of what is acceptable. Thus contrived virtue distorts the basal desire to be made right with God into an egocentric pretense that one can make oneself right by repressing whatever is unacceptable to oneself. In this sense, it is the height of self-deception and the epitome of faulty fulfillment.

As Freud's theory implies, repression as contrived virtue is no real solution to one's sense of unrighteousness. It is a temporary release that yields a timeless captivity. It grants an appearance of

4. Dietrich Bonhoeffer, *Ethics*, ed. Eberhard Bethge, trans. Neville H. Smith (New York: Macmillan, 1955), 26.

goodness but results in a condition of lasting enslavement. It promises deliverance but actually becomes the occasion of increased feelings of guilt.

A Life of Insatiable Demands

The attempt of persons to make themselves acceptable takes a third form. It can be called a life of insatiable demands and is illustrated by Mrs. Demand when she struggles with the tendency to live by what "ought to be" rather than by what actually is. Karen Horney's theory of personality can help us understand the psychological dynamics.

According to Horney, if persons live in an environment that makes it difficult for them to pursue their unique needs and possibilities, they may initiate a substitute process of growth to provide them with some sense of inner unity and outer relatedness. The substitute process, called neurosis, represents a change in direction in the core of the personality. Instead of trying to actualize their real potentialities, individuals strive to realize an unlimited and glorified version of themselves, at first in a visionary way through the creation of an idealized image but soon in a total and concrete way by trying to idealize everything they are and do. In other words, the attitude of idealization infiltrates their aspirations, their goals, their conduct of life, and their relation to others. It is a comprehensive search for glory in which they reach for the absolute—"[their] will power should have magic proportions, [their] reasoning be infallible, [their] foresight flawless, [their] knowledge all encompassing."[5]

However much neurotics seek to idealize themselves, they cannot escape reality completely, for both the limitations of their own being and the actualities of the impinging world remind them that their life has not been ordered completely according to the wishes of infinite realization. According to Horney, the neurotic has two ways to muffle the message of reality: the first, effective against the actualities of the world, is called "neurotic claims"; the second, effective against the limitations of self, is called "the tyranny of the should." It is the second way that attracts our attention.

5. Karen Horney, *Neurosis and Human Growth: The Struggle Toward Self-Realization* (New York: W. W. Norton, 1950), 34.

"The tyranny of the shoulds" refers to insatiable inner dictates that operate on the premise "that nothing should be, or is, impossible for oneself."[6] They are completely insensitive to the actual conditions under which individuals can find genuine fulfillment. Instead their whole life revolves around what ought to be, for they are dominated by the relentless demand that they should be different and more perfect than they really are. The individual strives "to mold himself into a supreme being of his own making. He holds before his soul" the image of perfection and is tortured by what he "should be able to do, to be, to feel, to know."[7] In this sense, the shoulds are qualitatively different than genuine ideals, for they are permeated by a spirit of egoism and are dominated by a spirit of coercion. Instead of urging individuals toward the actualization of their real selves, they destroy spontaneous growth, disturb relationships with others, and force people to live a life of insatiable demands.

For Horney, the shoulds are part of a process of idealization that has its roots in an adverse psychological environment. Pastoral counseling indicates that the shoulds can also function as an antidote to the feeling of guilt, as a way to become right. In fact, to tyrannize oneself with shoulds seems to be a promising way to do something about being unacceptable, for it is a rejection of what one is and an affirmation of what one ought to be. It is a pervasive and demanding attempt to be perfect. Thus individuals give the appearance of living a moral and meritorious life, especially since any failure to live up to their high standards subjects them to an incriminating sense of self-condemnation. In this sense, they epitomize the attempt of persons to take matters into their own hands in order to make themselves acceptable. Where they fall short of perfection, they manifest the proper self-condemnation and strive relentlessly to achieve optimal acceptability.

All their efforts do not give them the victory. A life of insatiable demands is an endless search for righteousness, because it tends to increase rather than decrease the individual's feeling of "not measuring up." Any failure, no matter how small, brings with it an incriminating sense of guilt. More important, a life of tyrannical demands goes beyond the attempt to make oneself acceptable

6. Ibid., 68.
7. Ibid., 64.

and is actually a destructive and boundless pursuit of false fulfillment. In the language of Horney, it is a denial of the real self and
an attempt to mold one's finite life into infinite goodness. In
Paul's language it is zeal for the law, for it holds the law in high
regard and puts one's trust in one's compulsive attempt to keep it.
In actual fact it is a radical instance of self-righteousness for it is
a serious attempt to make oneself acceptable by being the ultimate actualization of an absolute and self-defined perfection. In
the end, it is an idolatrous house of cards, as Mrs. Demand found
out: "I can't save myself. I've tried. I've tried both ways: I've tried
to save myself by being what I should be, and I've tried to get rid
of myself. I can't do either one."

Conclusion

We have now examined three major ways in which individuals
try to make themselves acceptable to self, to others, and to God.
Each way serves an important function in the total process of self-
justification. A life of suffering attempts to pay the price of guilt; a
life of contrived virtue tries to create a facade of goodness, and a
life of insatiable demands tries to actualize a state of perfection.
Our discussion indicates that self-justification is no real solution
to unrighteousness. Consequently, the agony of not being right
persists. The need to be accepted and recreated remains. If the
need becomes intense, individuals may acknowledge their impotence and may seek help from someone beyond themselves.

Individuals who come to counseling for help do not necessarily
give up the attempt to justify themselves. On the contrary, they
are inclined to try to use counseling as a means of self-
justification, that is, as a distressing process which by its very
nature should lead to acceptance and fulfillment. Counseling
can be distorted very easily to serve this purpose. It can become a
convenient way to suffer or an effective way to refine one's facade
of goodness, or a demanding way to satisfy one's tyrannical
"shoulds." These attempts are as fruitless in counseling as they
are in life. They nullify the therapeutic intent of counseling and
fail to satisfy the individual's longing to be made right.

Counseling must deal with and seek to correct this situation. I
think pastoral counseling is in a unique position to do this, for its
heart and soul, the gospel of Christ, is concerned primarily about

the struggle to become right. It assures us that there is no need, indeed no way, to make ourselves right by our own efforts, that we are acceptable to God in spite of being unacceptable. As guilty persons, we have a difficult time accepting this message, no matter how often we have heard it. As Mrs. Demand says, "I know I am forgiven in my mind, but why can't I accept it? Why can't I believe it?" Pastoral counseling must help at this point. In fact, it can help us give up the feverish attempt "to do something." It must help us to receive something that we do not deserve. If it succeeds, it frees us from the tortuous process of self-justification and allows us to live in the abundance of new life.

11

Counseling and the Development of Responsibility

LeRoy Aden

Our understanding of human responsibility has been extended and enriched by modern psychotherapy. Sigmund Freud made a significant contribution by showing that we humans are much less free than we sometimes think. He discovered that many of our thoughts and deeds are products of genetic determinisms that originate in infantile repressions. His discovery has forced us to reconsider our tendency to hold persons responsible for actions over which they have no real control. Consequently, we have been more understanding of troubled people, for we have a deeper appreciation for the way in which they are victims and not just villains. This appreciation, of course, can be, and at times has been, taken so far that we have tended to rob the individual of all responsibility.

William Glasser tries to correct this error. He minimizes determinisms of the past and emphasizes the idea that counseling should promote and seek to increase the individual's sense of responsibility. In fact, for him being responsible and living a responsible life become the key to self-esteem and fulfillment.

While we may not agree with the whole of Glasser's position, we need to take his concern with responsibility seriously. I believe that responsibility is a helpful perspective from which to view the process of counseling. Effective counseling can be seen as growth in responsibility or, more precisely, as growth in the individual's understanding of, and capacity for, responsibility. As I see it, growth in responsibility is a threefold development.

Responsibility as Accountability

In the initial stages of counseling individuals usually understand responsibility in a limited and negative way. They equate it with accountability, and by accountability they mean being "on the carpet," deserving criticism and blame for what they have done or failed to do. A twenty-year-old woman named Joan illustrates the point.

Joan came from a family where happiness and success were given top priority. The father epitomized this striving by spending long hours away from home trying to climb the social and economic ladder. Underneath all the activity, the family sensed that they were not going to make it. In fact, the more they tried, the more their hopes turned to ashes. Unconsciously, the family had to make someone responsible for this failure. They turned on Joan, the youngest and most helpless member of the family, not in a direct way but by generalized innuendos: "Why are you always different than other people?" "Why don't you know what you want to do with your life?" "Why can't you make it in college?"

Gradually Joan began to accept the family's evaluation and started to see herself as the one who was responsible for the family's failure: "I am always letting the family down." "I always start something but never complete it." By these self-evaluations, Joan held herself accountable, whipping herself for not living up to harsh and unrealistic expectations.

For Joan, responsibility has been reduced to a moralistic sting synonymous with blameworthiness and experienced as a finger of judgment that points to the many ways in which she does not measure up.

Responsibility in this sense can be a heavy burden. Consequently, we usually try to mitigate its message. One of the means at our disposal is to limit the extent of our guilt by owning up to a lesser guilt in order to escape responsibility for a more incriminating fault. Both Joan and her family were masters of this maneuver. Her family held her responsible for being different and for not knowing what to do with her life. As a result it did not have to own up to its own deeper guilt, namely, its tendency to make an idol out of happiness and success. In the same way Joan held herself responsible for not completing what she started. She evaded the deeper judgment of living far below her potential, of being a self-degrading and self-destructive individual.

Joan's situation indicates that what seems to be genuine responsibility may actually be an escape from it. Seward Hiltner makes the same point from a different angle when he says that "responsibility can be subverted by exaggeration."[1] The individual may be overconscientious in a particular segment of life and thus avoid responsible behavior on another level. Hiltner cites the example of a fourteen-year-old girl who took over the care of her siblings and the family household after her mother died. Her behavior was helpful and necessary at the time, but in the long run it was an evasion of responsibility for her own life, because she came to use the family situation as an excuse for not developing her own gifts.

Effective counseling changes and deepens our understanding of responsibility in at least two ways. First, responsibility as accountability loses its moralistic sting. We turn from the tendency to whip ourselves with negative judgments and are able to assume genuine accountability for our real guilt. Joan, for example, moved away from the tendency to fall into destructive self-blame and became more and more able to own up to the fact that she was a small and frightened miniature of what she could become. She gained the strength to hold herself accountable for the part that she played in her plight without feeling totally crushed and condemned by it.

Second, effective counseling empowers us to become the focus of our own accountability. Instead of living by an externally imposed responsibility, we begin to hold ourselves accountable. We

1. Seward Hiltner, "Clinical and Theological Notes on Responsibility," *Journal of Religion and Health* 2, 1 (Oct. 1962): 9.

become our own judge. We become a center of evaluation and are able to call ourselves into question if and when it is appropriate.

Accountability in this revised sense is an elementary but very important way to understand responsibility. It underlines the fact that we are held accountable for the life given to us, if not by others then, we hope, by ourselves. Paul Tillich summarizes the point: A person's life "is not only given to him but also demanded of him. He is responsible for it; literally, he is required to answer, if he is asked, what he has made of himself. He who asks him is his judge, namely, he himself, who, at the same time, stands against him."[2]

Accountability, then, is a proper way to understand responsibility. It is a basic aspect of our existence. But accountability does not exhaust human responsibility. Experience gained in counseling practice indicates that there is a second and deeper dimension to it.

Responsibility as Response-Ability

As people progress in counseling, their sense of responsibility goes beyond mere accountability and becomes what can be called a sense of response-ability. They realize that they have the ability to choose from among alternatives, that they have the power to make things happen rather than to have things simply happen to them. They discover that, within limits, they can determine the shape and direction of their lives.

People who stand at this juncture have taken a giant step. They have moved beyond the elementary stance of holding themselves accountable for actions already completed and have discovered that they are active centers of autonomy and self-determination. They are responsible in the sense that they are intentional in their deliberations and decisions. To be responsible in this sense means to own up to the reality of one's finite freedom. It means to become more fully and more self-consciously responsive to one's total situation.

Joan is a concrete example. She got to a point where she no longer reacted to the family milieu with an automatic sense of guilt and self-doubt. She began to see that she could respond to

2. Paul Tillich, *The Courage To Be* (New Haven: Yale University Press, 1952), 51.

her situation in a number of different ways. For example, her reaction to the accusations of the family could range from unquestioned acceptance to open rejection. Likewise, she realized that college might not be a viable means of fulfillment for her, no matter how much the family might want her to go, so she did not need to react with automatic acquiescence. Finally, she discovered that the real question for her was not "What do they think I should do with my life?" but "What do I want to do with it?" In a multitude of ways, Joan became more responsible by becoming more responsive to self, others, and one hopes, God. She was aware of herself as an agent of action and could begin to take charge of her life in spite of possible consequences.

Joan's experience indicates that the move toward responseability is a move toward the present. Unlike responsibility as accountability, which tends to be oriented toward the past, toward what the individual has done or been, responsibility as the ability to respond is oriented toward the contemporary moment. It focuses on the self as an active responder in an existing field of current possibilities. It is the existential recognition of "I can" and in some sense "I must." This recognition brings with it both exhilaration and dread—exhilaration because it releases the person from the bondage of the predetermined response, dread because it may end in failure and thus burden the individual with guilt. In any case, the individual soon learns that his or her response-ability is not absolute or unconditioned. He or she always exercises it in the context of history, in which multifarious forces have shaped and continue to shape him or her. H. Richard Niebuhr makes the same point from a slightly different angle: "We respond as we interpret the meaning of actions upon us. . . . Such interpretation, it need scarcely be added, is not simply an affair of our conscious, and rational, mind but also of the deep memories that are buried within us, of feelings and intuitions that are only partly under our immediate control."[3]

Being responsible in the sense of being free to respond in a variety of ways is a significant achievement. It opens up all kinds of possibilities for the individual. Ironically, one of the possibilities that it introduces is the possibility that there is more to responsibility than simply the ability to respond. The individual

3. H. Richard Niebuhr, *The Responsible Self* (New York: Harper, 1963), 63.

who pursues this possibility experiences responsibility in a third and decisive way.

Responsibility as Fitting Response

Individuals in counseling may celebrate their increased response-ability, but they soon discover that it is not a resting place. As they exercise their ability to respond they inevitably make inadequate or even faulty choices which tend to distort rather than to fulfill them. Consequently, they begin to see the necessity of making deliberate and discreet decisions. They begin to realize that they must struggle with the question, "What is the proper response? What is the fitting thing to do as far as self and others are concerned?" To struggle with this question is to be responsible in the fullest sense of the word. In fact, the struggle is crucial to individuals; otherwise, they will not maintain the freedom they have achieved or experience the fulfillment they desire.

Arriving at a fitting response is not a matter of being perfect and, therefore, infallible. In the process of counseling, clients see through that demand as an undesirable and impossible goal. They realize that making a right response is a matter of being released and empowered, released from blind inattention to be able to see the situation as it is and empowered with the wisdom to respond to it in a way that is both appropriate and enhancing. Joan, for example, will never respond if she must wait until she comes up with the perfect response. To live by that expectation would actually be a form of irresponsibility. Instead she must act in the midst of complexity and uncertainty, knowing that the situation is made up of many conflicting factors and granting that there may be a number of more or less fitting responses. She can only approximate the optimal, but the approximation demonstrates her maturity and is crucial to her long-term fulfillment.

Niebuhr puts the point in a larger framework. He maintains that man has used two basic images to understand himself as an agent of action: the image of "maker" and the image of "citizen." "Man as maker" refers to our power to create, to our ability both to act with an end in mind and, within limits, to fashion and give form to ourselves. "Man as citizen" refers to our self-imposed discipline, to our ability to create and to give ourselves to rules and laws for the sake of order and justice. Niebuhr implies that responsibility can be understood from either perspective, but he is concerned to develop a third image. He maintains that we are also answerers, that we are creatures in constant dialogue who act in response to action upon us. This image of us highlights the interactional nature of responsibility. Specifically, in any moment of deliberation and decision we are more or less attentive to the impinging situation, whether internal or external. We ask, consciously or unconsciously, "What is going on?" or, more personally, "What is being done to me?" Our interpretation of that situation helps us to address the crucial question: "What is a fitting response to what is happening? What is an appropriate reply?" The person who answers that question accurately is the person who is truly responsible. Niebuhr clarifies why: "The *fitting* action, the one that fits into a total interaction as response and an anticipation of further response, is alone conducive to the good and alone is right."[4]

The individual who is able to be responsible in Niebuhr's sense is living toward the future. The fitting response is actualized in the present, but it anticipates and contributes to the individual's long-term fulfillment. It transcends past accountability and the plethora of present possibilities, and represents a discriminate response that tends to enhance the individual's continuing participation in future interactions. It is the point at which the individual stands above the multitude of factors that impinge upon him or her and, within limits, is able to decide the direction and shape of his or her life. To respond in this way is the epitome of human freedom and the fullness of human responsibility.

Conclusion

Counseling revitalizes the concept of responsibility. "You are responsible" ceases to be a charge of condemnation and becomes a recognition of growth and fulfillment. It means that we have achieved an increased capacity to own up to our faults, to exercise our finite freedom, and to respond to our situation in a fitting way. To be responsible in this sense is a marvelous gift. It is a realization of our human nature. It is an anticipation of our human destiny.

4. Ibid., 61.

PART 3

Forgiveness

12

Punitive and Reconciliation Models of Forgiveness

E. MANSELL PATTISON

This chapter examines the psychodynamics of forgiveness and the pathologies that interfere with the process of forgiveness. Forgiveness has been primarily a theological concern, regarded as alien to psychotherapy but of central concern to religion. This is illustrated by Paul Meehl's[1] survey in which both pastors and psychologists were concerned with guilt, but pastors alone reported concern with forgiveness. Andras Angyal[2] is one of the few psychologists who has described forgiveness as relevant to both therapist and cleric, and both Paul Tournier and John G. McKenzie[3] have attempted cohesive statements on guilt and forgiveness. In this chapter we want to address the relative neglect of forgiveness from a psychological perspective. Specifically we want to consider not just the psychopathology of forgiveness but, more important, we want to present a systematic model of forgiveness, a model based on existential concepts and relevant to both psychology and theology.

1. Paul Meehl, ed., *What, Then, Is Man?* (St. Louis: Concordia, 1958).
2. Andras Angyal, "The Convergence of Psychotherapy and Religion," *Journal of Pastoral Care* 5 (1951) 4: 4–14.
3. Paul Tournier, *Guilt and Grace* (New York: Harper, 1962); John G. McKenzie, *Guilt: Its Meaning and Significance* (Nashville: Abingdon, 1962).

The Development of Forgiveness

In personality development the need for forgiveness arises as a consequence of guilt. Guilt is grounded in fear, and fear stems from the ambivalence of the early child-parent relationship. Children are self-centered persons, so when the parent begins to impose disciplinary restrictions they feel frustrated and become angry. They are ambivalent about whether to accept the satisfaction of parental approval or to gratify their selfish interests. They hate the parent for being restrictive and fear retaliation for both breaking the rules and being angry. All restrictions are seen as punishment, because children are too young to perceive motivations. Besides, the violation of rules produces a degree of condemnation and punishment in the parent. The condemnation by the parent is reinforced by the child's own frustrated anger which he or she deflects from the parent to the self to avoid provoking further parental retaliation. These two sources of anger—the parent and the child—become internalized as the child's superego.

The child seeks forgiveness to relieve the guilt of infantile gratification, but this is a mechanistic pattern of forgiveness. The parent is not a person but an object. In Martin Buber's terms, the model is an "I-It," rather than an "I-Thou," relationship.[4] The resolution of guilt is by punishment, not forgiveness. Therefore, I call this a punitive model of forgiveness, which is not forgiveness at all but only the payment of a price for narcissistic merchandise.

Gradually the child develops what Jean Piaget calls "moral realism."[5] With maturation children develop relationships with their parents as persons. They realize that guilt does not refer to acts but to underlying attitudes, that the anxiety is not over punishment but over estrangement. The driving force for the resolution of guilt becomes the deprivation of love. Identification with parental expectations becomes internalized as the ego ideal. Thus violations do not produce guilt, but instead elicit shame, that is, fear of parental contempt and abandonment.

The process of forgiveness involves reconciliation in the I-Thou of love. This is different than the previously established superego

4. Martin Buber, *I and Thou* (New York: Scribners, 1958).
5. Jean Piaget, *The Moral Judgment of the Child* (New York: Harcourt, 1932).

condemnation that leads the child to anticipate punishment as the requisite to forgiveness. Yet no payment or sacrifice will bring forgiveness; one can only seek to reestablish the I-Thou relationship. Likewise, the one who forgives can only accept back the one who is forgiven into a love relationship. If the forgiver demands payment, he or she is violating the I-Thou relationship by using it to gratify his or her need to retaliate for being offended in the first place. I call this a reconciliation model of forgiveness. It involves the conscious willfulness of forgiver and forgiven to seek reunion. In it the punitive element remains as only an anachronistic reflection of a hostile, rather than of a loving, relationship.

Forgiveness is the completed act of reconciliation between the guilty one and the offended one. It involves six steps: guilt, confession, remorse, restitution, mutual acceptance, and reconciliation. Pathological failures can occur at every step of the process.

The Nature of Guilt

Guilt presupposes responsibility. No forgiveness can occur until the proper responsibility is assumed. If guilt is incorrectly assessed, it is pseudoguilt and can never lead to proper responsibility and real forgiveness.

Buber discerns three spheres of guilt:

1. the laws of society;
2. religious faith, and
3. the sphere of conscience.[6]

Guilt in the first sphere has no place for forgiveness. It is determined by objective definition, and the model for forgiveness is a punitive one—a specific infraction carries specific penalties. Religious or personal guilt is entirely extraneous to this state of guilt, for civil guilt is arbitrary and bears no necessary relationship to morality. The martyrs to Nazi justice testify to this.

David E. Roberts speaks of civil versus religious guilt in Søren Kierkegaard's terms: Civil guilt is punitive; religious guilt is restorative.[7] Religiously, one cannot pay for guilt by taking a lick-

---

6. Martin Buber, "Guilt and Guilt Feelings," *Psychiatry* 20 (1957): 117–50.
7. David E. Roberts, *Existentialism and Religious Belief* (New York: Oxford, 1957).

ing, for forgiveness is an attitude and state, not something earned. Religious or existential guilt is also objective. It refers to our estrangement from God, the denial of our true situation, and our aspiration to be our own deity. Existential guilt, as defined by Søren Kierkegaard, Medard Boss, Paul Tillich, and Jean Paul Sartre,[8] is the essence of our situation. It is not a feeling but a situation that arouses ontological anxiety or dreadful fear (*Urangst*).

Rollo May notes that ontological guilt, if unaccepted and repressed, may turn into neurotic guilt.[9] If true, when we attempt to obtain forgiveness for our existential guilt we fail, because the neurotic pseudoguilt hides our estrangement from God. Otto Rank, too, makes a distinction between moralistic and ethical guilt, pointing out that the punitive demands of conscience may lead to stifling compliance with morals that prevents us from seeing the fundamental ethical or religious imperative.[10] This is "pharisaism" at its ultimate, for "the letter [of the law] kills, but the spirit gives life" (2 Cor. 3:6).

According to Wilfred Daim and Medard Boss, the task of psychotherapy is to divest patients of neurotic subjective guilt so that they can responsibly face their existential guilt.[11] Victor Frankl's Logotherapy addresses itself precisely to this existential predicament,[12] while Buber holds that existential guilt and forgiveness lie beyond the competence of the psychotherapist. The Christian faith claims that our estrangement from God and from our own true being can never be ameliorated by therapy but only through experiencing the forgiveness of God. The existentialist would agree that the elimination of neurotic subjective guilt leads to no necessary existential forgiveness. Successful psycho-

---

8. Roberts, *Existentialism and Religious Belief;* Medard Boss, *Psychoanalysis and Daseinanalysis,* trans. Ludwig B. Lefebre (New York: Basic, 1963); Leon Salzman, "Observations on Dr. Tillich's Views on Guilt, Sin, and Reconciliation," *Journal of Pastoral Care* 11 (Spring 1957): 14–19; Jean Paul Sartre, *Existentialism and Human Emotions* (New York: Philosophical Library, 1958).

9. Rollo May, Ernest Angel, and Henri F. Ellenberger, eds., *Existence* (New York: Basic, 1958).

10. Otto Rank, *Art and Artist* (New York: Knopf, 1932).

11. Wilfred Daim, *Depth Psychology and Salvation* (New York: Unger, 1963); Boss, *Psychoanalysis and Daseinanalysis.*

12. Victor Frankl, *Man's Search for Meaning: An Introduction to Logotherapy* (Boston: Beacon, 1962).

analysis is no guarantee of a forgiven person. As a corollary I hold that existential forgiveness occurs in the face of, and despite, obvious failure to resolve neurotic subjective guilt in the neurotic and even in the psychotic.

The third sphere of guilt is subjective rather than objective. It is an affect, a feeling of guilt. As John G. McKenzie points out, such guilt is always neurotic in that it reflects the failure either to mature beyond the punitive model or to resolve the ambivalent self-desires of the reconciliation model. Such guilt, says Sandor Rado,[13] is always a sign that reparations must be made and is never a signal for preventive action.

Neurotic guilt is based on the punitive model and leads to neurotic anxiety. In the reconciliation model we also find anxiety, but it can be used constructively according to one's ideals and values by being motivated by concern rather than by fear.

To this point we have considered pathologies of forgiveness in terms of the three spheres of guilt. Now let us consider pathologies arising from confusion between the punitive and reconciliation models of forgiveness.

Ernest Jones observed that the guilt of the punitive model is poorly tolerated in the person, who defends himself against it with fear or hate.[14] If the defense is fear the guilty person may develop physiological reactions, either anxiety attacks or psychosomatic states. If the defense is hate the original hostility may lead to murder, the ultimate failure to forgive others; or, if the hostility is turned upon the self, it may lead to suicide, the ultimate failure to forgive oneself. The superego never forgives; it can only be satiated.

The punitive model reflects a narcissistic, self-centered interest. The sociopathic character, as typified in the chronic criminal, is characteristic of the punitive model. Sociopaths are said to have no guilt and never seek forgiveness. This is true in that they have an I-It model where persons are of value only for what they can give. They experience anxiety and fear lest they not get what they want or be punished for trying to get it. But they have no

13. Sandor Rado, "Emergency Behavior: With an Introduction to the Dynamics of Conscience," in *Psychoanalysis and Behavior* (New York: Grune and Stratton, 1956).

14. Ernest Jones, "Fear, Guilt, and Hate," *Papers on Psychoanalysis* (Boston: Beacon, 1961).

I-Thou capacity, no ability to experience personal estrangement from love and no desire for forgiveness.

The punitive model can never lead to true forgiveness, for it sees I-Thou guilt in terms of I-It relationships. Consequently, persons with punitive, infantile superegos may attempt to placate the demands for punishment as a misguided attempt to obtain forgiveness. They may indeed placate the superego, but they have not obtained forgiveness for they are operating at the wrong level of human existence.

These misguided attempts are responsible for much of the neurotic and psychotic pathology that we see as a result of guilt. O. Hobart Mowrer is partly correct when he insists that psychological disease stems from real guilt, that is, from real events in our lives.[15] The punitive superego does not discriminate between those events that call for forgiveness and those that do not. Forgiveness is not a superego phenomenon. So when Mowrer ignores these distinctions he misapprehends forgiveness and his prescriptions for forgiveness are misapplied.

Charles Odier, a French Catholic psychoanalyst, has described both the conscious and unconscious aspects of neurotic guilt.[16] Unconscious guilt results from repression in an effort to dispel the guilt rather than to obtain forgiveness—an attempt to have one's cake and eat it too! This repression of the superego leads to psychological symptoms, as Mowrer maintains.

A decade before Mowrer, John C. Flugel had outlined the neurotic mechanisms by which a person evades superego guilt:

1. Reparation, or the payment of penalties as typified in the obsessive-compulsive neurotic who slaps his own wrist for misbehavior
2. Confession, or the acknowledgment of guilt as self-punishment or as a superego bribe to continue guilty behavior
3. Repression, or the loss of guilt to consciousness which creates anxiety and the formation of neurotic symptoms

15. O. Hobart Mowrer, *The Crisis in Psychiatry and Religion* (Princeton: Van Nostrand, 1961).

16. Charles Odier, *Les Deux Sources, Consciento et Inconsciente, de la Via Morale* (Neuchatel: De la Baconniere, 1943).

4. Projection, or the shifting of blame to others which reaches its ultimate expression in paranoid psychosis
5. Rationalization, or the justification of one's guilty behavior[17]

Each of these mechanisms may effectively dissipate conscious guilt at the expense of neurotic symptoms, but unconsciously the guilt remains and forgiveness never ensues. Forgiveness starts with the apprehension of appropriate guilt in terms of the appropriate model; otherwise, the process of forgiveness never commences in either a religious or a psychological sense.

The Nature of Confession

Confession is the prelude to forgiveness and the recognition of personal responsibility. It is the perception of estrangement in the I-Thou relationship and the acknowledgment of one's initiative in violating that relationship. Effective confession leads one to pursue remedial steps to reestablish the I-Thou relationship.

Confession may be used to deny responsibility rather than to affirm it. In Alcoholics Anonymous (AA) persons admit that they are helpless within the clutches of a disease, but they need feel no responsibility. The denial of responsibility leads to a continued symbiotic dependence on AA rather than bringing the alcoholic to a condition of self-acceptance and mature responsibility. In a recent family treatment project in the Cincinnati Alcoholism Clinic, we repeatedly observed families who were willing to confess to helplessness in dealing with overwhelming reality problems. They asked the visiting nurse to help them out of their helplessness but were enraged when the nurse tried to help them accept responsibility for dealing with their own predicament. Confession was a way out but not a way up.

Confession may be masochistic, a relentless exposure of one's faults to gain the attention, sympathy, and love of others. This is the hostile, controlling maneuver based on self-gratification that Theodor Reik describes in *The Compulsion to Confess*.[18] A husband in marital group therapy came every week to proclaim that

17. John C. Flugel, *Man, Morals, and Society* (New York: Viking, 1961).
18. Theodor Reik, *The Compulsion to Confess* (New York: Farrar, Straus, and Cudahy, 1959).

the marital problems were all his fault; he liked to detail his failures as a husband. His confession invited attention rather than forgiveness.

Confession, notes Leon Salzman,[19] can be used to diminish responsibility or punishment; it acts as a defense against acknowledging true guilt. Instead it acknowledges pseudoguilt and is ineffectual. For example, in civil court a person may confess to a lesser crime in order to avert conviction and a more severe penalty. In AA alcoholics may give a stock confession of their drinking so that they do not have to confess to their omnipotent fantasies, their shame of inadequacy, and their anger at frustration.

A person may also confess to the group as a means of making them share guilt. For example, a husband in marital group therapy confessed his shortcomings within the group and no longer felt guilty because the group registered no disapproval. He mistook group acceptance for group approval. The confession was also a disarming mechanism, for his wife could not upbraid him in the face of his having "come clean" in front of everybody.

The most obvious distortion of confession is the "scrupulosity syndrome." Scrupulous persons are bothered by incessant feelings of guilt and depression over their religious behavior. They seek confession repetitively but obtain no feeling of relief. Often this pattern is considered a Catholic problem, but I will describe a Protestant case of it.

The patient was a thirty-year-old Holiness minister who found it increasingly difficult to preach because he felt hypocritical. He demanded perfection of himself because holiness meant making absolutely no mistakes. He dreaded the one mistake that would send him plunging to hell. He prayed incessantly but found no forgiveness. He wept at the altar rail to no avail. He hated himself for failing and experienced dread anxiety before each sermon. At other times, he felt that he could achieve a flawless existence superior to any of his colleagues. During therapy he revealed hatred toward his alcoholic father whom he projected as God, demanding perfection. He desired perfection as an omnipotent identification with the Father-God, while simultaneously he hated the Father-God for demanding what he could not be.

19. Salzman, "Observations on Dr. Tillich's Views."

The crux of the scrupulosity problem is the pseudoguilt for specific acts which obscures the defiant hostility toward the ambivalent parental figure. Confession of the acts is a defense against the recognition of the attitude.

Flugel has observed that Protestantism has exchanged the tyranny of the external superego of the Catholic Church for the greater tyranny of the individual's internal superego.[20] Gordon W. Allport and Mowrer both speak of the return of the Protestant confessional as a therapeutic boon.[21] But Carroll A. Wise wonders if standardized ritual will not lead to structuralized guilt.[22] Earl A. Loomis notes that we want acceptance but not restoration.[23] Andras Angyal says that we want to feel better, not be better, learning to sin without getting punished or having to maintain a relationship with anyone.[24]

In many Holiness churches the altar rail has been a masochistic wailing wall, and in many confessionals only the superego has been appeased. The confessional placates but cannot reconcile. One patient of mine returned from confession criticizing the cleric for not imposing severe penance. He felt he had been robbed of the chance to absolve his guilt! Confession is a first step, but as Samuel Novey warns, it may use institutionalized forms of confession as a neurotic defense.

The Nature of Remorse

Although confession may mean acknowledgment and acceptance of responsibility, sorrow, remorse, or contrition for behavior need not follow. I have seen many sociopaths defiantly confess and readily accept responsibility for their behavior. They are sorry that they got caught but not sorry for what they did.

Genuine remorse is the recognition of the hostility expressed toward the Thou, and the desire to be reconciled in love. It is not self-condemnation as an attempt to extract sympathy, nor is it a wallowing in self-pity. As Victor White notes, contrition is the op-

20. Flugel, *Man, Morals, and Society*, 146–51.

21. Gordon W. Allport, *The Individual and His Religion*, (New York: Macmillan, 1950); O. Hobart Mowrer, *The New Group Therapy* (Princeton: Van Nostrand, 1964).

22. Caroll A. Wise, *Pastoral Counseling* (New York: Harper, 1951).

23. Earl A. Loomis, *The Self in Pilgrimage* (New York: Harper, 1960).

24. Andras Angyal, "The Convergence of Psychotherapy and Religion," *Journal of Pastoral Care* 5 (1951): 4–14.

posite of obsessive remorse.[25] It is an objective appraisal of one's state, not the punitive condemnation of one's behavior. In this sense it is the motivating spur to reconstitutive action rather than the occasion for punitive self-flagellation. But if one is operating by the punitive model of forgiveness remorse is turning on oneself with anger that was originally directed at the frustrating person. Hence, depression and suicide reflect the failure to see the true path to forgiveness.

True remorse is not regret. Sociopaths regret their actions because they do not get what they want, but they suffer no remorse because they have no person other than themselves from whom to be estranged.

The Nature of Restitution

It is here that the distinction between the punitive and the reconciliation models of forgiveness is most clearly seen. In the punitive model, restitution is a payment to avoid retaliation. Marc Oraison describes how this practice fails to grasp the nature of sin, for sin is a relational concept.[26] In the reconciliation model, restitution for sin is the reestablishment of the condition of the I-Thou relationship. If I have stolen your purse and then seek forgiveness I must return the purse, not because I will not otherwise be forgiven or because it is demanded by the forgiver. Rather, I return the purse because my love compels me to restore what belongs to you. To keep the purse is self-serving and repudiates my love for you, so restitution consists of returning anything I have taken from you.

Restitution does not always constitute a condition of forgiveness. It is meaningful only if it reflects the attitude toward the relationship. Mechanical replacement is meaningless to forgiveness. Furthermore, the sin may involve nothing to be restituted. To demand restitution if it is impossible or undesirable is to respond to the punitive impulses within oneself. It is a failure to acknowledge the fact that love accepts one as one is.

Restitution is in no way either a punishment or a "making up." Yet it is often distorted in these ways, serving as a block to forgive-

25. Victor White, "Guilt: Theological and Psychological," *Christian Essays in Psychiatry*, ed. Philip Mairet (New York: Philosophical Library, 1956), 175.
26. Marc Oraison, ed., *Sin: A Symposium* (New York: Macmillan, 1962), 18–19.

ness. The obsessive-compulsive neurotic is a good example. One of my patients slaps her mouth when she starts to say a forbidden word, becomes apologetic, and makes absurd offers to make up for allegedly hurting me. She tries to undo her actions like a child trying to piece together a broken plate she dropped. These attempts at restitution are based on narcissism. As William E. Hulme points out, my patient is attempting self-atonement without realizing that I accept her as she is.

The attempt to undo one's actions is a neurotic failure to distinguish between punitive demands and the need for reconciliation. Again, a good example is Alcoholics Anonymous. In the "Twelfth Step" of the AA program alcoholics are to repay others as they are able, going out to help others who are alcoholic. This continual repayment in time and energy is an attempt to undo the past, negate one's condition, and prove by present activity the falseness of the past. Furthermore, the rescue activities play upon the rescue fantasies of the dependent alcoholic who saves himself vicariously by saving others.

The psychological structure of AA depends upon denial of responsibility, shared group guilt, a continued undoing neurosis, and a rescue fantasy. The need for continued AA affiliation is exactly true, because it is the perpetuation of a neurosis. This is not meant to deprecate AA, for it is a tremendous ally against alcoholism and I have seen individuals mature psychologically in AA. But I have also seen individuals remain psychologically fixated and symbiotically dependent on AA. Research reports indicate that the AA cure is often the exchange of an alcoholic neurosis for an AA neurosis. This is a worthy gain, but I cannot agree with David Belgum, O. Hobart Mowrer, Howard J. Clinebell, and Wayne E. Oates that this is a model of forgiveness.[27]

Neither can I agree with Thomas J. Bigham's attempt to find theological justification for punishment as a part of restitution.[28] As Warren C. Quanbeck points out, we are reluctant to see forgive-

27. David Belgum, *Guilt: Where Psychology and Religion Meet* (Englewood Cliffs, N.J.: Prentice-Hall, 1963); Mowrer, *The New Group Therapy;* Howard J. Clinebell, *Understanding and Counseling the Alcoholic Through Religion and Psychology,* (Nashville: Abingdon, 1956); Wayne E. Oates, *Protestant Pastoral Counseling* (Philadelphia: Westminster, 1962).

28. Thomas J. Bigham, "Redemption Through Punishment," *Journal of Pastoral Care* 12 (1958): 149–58.

ness as purely a function of love.[29] Restitution never implies punishment. Leon Morris presents a biblical exegesis of wrath and judgment which, he says, refers not to divine hostility but to the settled opposition of holiness to evil.[30] We anthropomorphize God's personality and project the punitiveness of our superego onto him. Bernard G. Meyerson and Louis Stoller, looking at the crucifixion psychoanalytically, aptly note that the cross stands as a warning to us that we are narcissistic creatures with an inability, actually a fear, to love.[31] We would rather take punishment than admit to Christ's demand for total love and accept that love as the measure of forgiveness.

The Nature of Mutual Acceptance

The guilty person goes through the previous steps by himself, but now the process must include the forgiver as well. Here we see the pathology of the failure to forgive in contrast to the failure to be forgiven. As we will see, the failure to forgive others is ultimately the failure to forgive oneself.

In forgiveness, the guilty one accepts the implication of dependence on the love of the other. Unqualified love is threatening because it highlights the nature of our inadequacies. Children sometimes repudiate the advance of love because they fear the implication of surrendering their rebellious autonomy. They fear becoming slaves of their loving parents rather than seeing the nurturing growth available within that love.

In forgiveness the forgiver must share the guilt, anguish, and estrangement of the sinner. To forgive is to extend one's love to the one who has violated it, but this can only be done genuinely as one experiences the meaning of that separation. McKenzie describes the process by referring to the mother who begins to feel the estrangement of, and from, the naughty child but who nevertheless goes to envelop the child in her arms.[32]

Loomis points out that to accept another, one must accept one-

29. Warren C. Quanbeck, "Forgiveness," *The Interpreter's Dictionary of the Bible*, ed. Arthur Buttrick et al. (Nashville: Abingdon, 1962).

30. Leon Morris, *The Biblical Doctrine of Judgment* (Grand Rapids: Eerdmans, 1960).

31. Bernard G. Meyerson and Louis Stoller, "A Psychoanalytic Interpretation of the Crucifixion," *Psychoanalysis and Psychoanalytic Review* 49 (1962): 117–18.

32. McKenzie, *Guilt*, 165.

self.[33] To identify with the guilty person implies that one accepts the feeling of guilt in oneself. This may be blocked by the self-righteousness of the forgiver. One may demand the "pound of flesh" as the condition of forgiveness. One may refuse to forgive the truly penitent as a hostile retaliation, making him or her suffer. One may forgive as duty, which is a condescending gesture. In all these instances one is gratifying the narcissistic desire to retaliate. Forgiveness is a facade. It is a receipt for payment but not a reconciliation.

The failure to forgive may possess deeper dynamics. One may refuse to forgive so as to provoke anger again in the penitent. This gives the forgiver justification to retaliate rather than to forgive. In marital group therapy our couples are so threatened by the reality of loving dependency on each other that they provoke attacks and refuse to forgive, so that they can maintain justified anger rather than admit their longing for love.

Another pattern is the need to forgive others. This is a masochistic maneuver aimed at gratifying one's omnipotence. This person goes about getting hurt by others so that he can magnanimously forgive and demonstrate his lovingkindness. Every church has at least one such morally masochistic wife who demonstrates her saintly ability to forgive an alcoholic husband for thirty years, although she unwittingly provokes him to offend her. The wife keeps her husband an alcoholic so that she can maintain her masochistic forgiving role.

Another pathology is the omnipotent person who aspires to perfection, which usually means the renunciation of many desires and impulses. "Unforgiving legalists," Oates calls them.[34] They cannot tolerate imperfection in others who are like themselves. They cannot forgive themselves or accept themselves as imperfect. They are particularly intolerant of others who do accept themselves because of their apparent self-indulgence.

One may fail to forgive because of one's own guilt. The offender is a convenient target for minimizing one's own guilt by making the other person appear more guilty. This is scapegoating. Pro-

33. Earl A. Loomis, "Superego and Values," *Religion in the Developing Personality* (New York: Academy of Religion and Mental Health, 1960).

34. Wayne E. Oates, *Religious Factors in Mental Illness* (London: Allen and Unwin, 1957).

jecting one's own guilt onto another person allows one to punish them instead of oneself. Such is the course of prejudice.

One can also be too forgiving, denying the other person's guilt, minimizing or forgetting it. This occurs when we fear rejection by the guilty one, for example, a child who readily excuses the parent for an obvious offense. Ready forgiveness may be a defense against one's actual anger and wish for retaliation, or it may be a masochistic self-punishment.

Mutual acceptance does not overlook the gravity of estrangement, or seek payment or punishment, or use the occasion for self-gratification. It is the mutual realization of the I-Thou estrangement and the mutual yearning for reunion.

The Nature of Reconciliation

Reconciliation is the completed act of restoration to an I-Thou relationship. The punitive model of forgiveness, based upon superego morality, can never lead to reconciliation, for in the I-It model only the self exists. Superego morality produces neurotic guilt feelings which impede the resolution of I-Thou violations in both the psychological and theological spheres.

Both personal and spiritual forgiveness are contingent upon mutual recognition and reconciliation between two people. Gerhart Piers and Milton B. Singer[35] have amplified Heinz Hartmann's ego psychology[36] to describe the maturational drive in the personality that leaves behind superego guilt and ego ideal shame and learns to establish an ego model for forgiveness. The establishment of autonomous ego values allows one to react to others in terms of one's actual moral commitments, freed from the obligation to act upon infantile desires.[37] Realistic anxiety aroused by estrangement is constructive anxiety as it spurs forgiver and forgiven to appropriate moral action. Therefore true forgiveness is a conscious process involving both the forgiver and the forgiven. This is ego morality. As such, one makes the conscious decision

35. Gerhart Piers and Milton B. Singer, *Shame and Guilt* (Springfield, Ill.: Thomas, 1957).

36. Heinz Hartmann, *Essays on Ego Psychology* (New York: International Universities Press, 1963).

37. Heinz Hartmann, *Psychoanalysis and Moral Values* (New York: International Universities Press, 1960).

not to choose retaliation but to seek restoration of the I-Thou relationship. Donald S. Browning describes the love of forgiveness as enduring the hostility of sin and remaining unqualified in its capacity to receive the guilty one back into relationship.[38]

Superego guilt says "I feel guilty" whereas ego guilt says "I am guilty." The punitive model of forgiveness applies to the first; the reconciliation model to the second. Theology and psychology overlap in that they share the reconciliation model, as both Joseph Havens and Angyal stress.[39] The therapist accepts the patient as he is and forgives the patient for being what he is; that is, the therapist accepts the patient in a relationship regardless of the patient's condition. Later the patient forgives the therapist for not being the ideal figure the patient desired. Eventually therapist and patient may come to a conscious mutuality of recognition and acceptance. In reconciliation forgiveness, the acceptance is already present in parent, therapist, and God, waiting to be accepted by the child, patient, and sinner. The state of forgiveness is waiting; the forgiven person need only enter into that state.

Salzman defines guilt as the hostile, defiant, rejecting attitude toward authority, one's own integrity, and one's true being.[40] Daim emphasizes that psychoanalysis addresses itself to feeling guilty and achieves a "partial salvation."[41] Total salvation comes with the reconciliation of existential estrangement. Failure to deal with neurotic guilt leads to punitive model forgiveness as manifested in neurosis and psychosis. It prevents one from facing the existential guilt of either psychology or theology. Conversely, failure to deal with existential psychological guilt or ontological theological guilt leads to neurotic guilt.

38. Donald S. Browning, "A Doctrine of the Atonement Informed by the Psychotherapeutic Process," *Journal of Pastoral Care* 17 (1963): 136–47.

39. Joseph Havens, "Psychotherapy and Salvation," *Pastoral Psychology* 12 (1961): 10–18; Angyal, "Convergence."

40. Salzman, "Observations on Dr. Tillich's Views."

41. Daim, *Depth Psychology and Salvation.*

13

Forgiveness and Human Relationships

LYMAN T. LUNDEEN

In a Christian frame of reference, forgiveness is often seen as the very center of faith. It stands as the ultimate cornerstone on which all other claims rest. In my own Lutheran tradition, there are many theologians who sound like Vince Lombardi when he said, "Winning is not the most important thing. It's the *only* thing." For these theologians forgiveness is the only thing. Their intention is not to say that there are no other issues in theology but to make sure that forgiveness is at the very center of life, shaping and coloring all other realities. Forgiveness does not eliminate other features of reality, like pain or loss or obligations, but it puts everything else in proper perspective and keeps them out of the center.

Forgiveness is a decisive reality for those who embrace the Christian faith, but it is not exclusive to them. It is a reality in the broad spectrum of human experience, and it can be described without explicit reference to any religious faith. Perhaps it is not real in the lives of people often enough or in profound or reliable ways, but people know of it when it is introduced as a way of resolving conflict or of mitigating loss. It is a down-to-earth experience that touches chords of memory or instills hope in most people.

Why does forgiveness make a decisive difference in human interaction? Why does it touch the fabric of human life to empower and transform it? For that matter, why does the Christian faith put such emphasis on forgiveness?

These are the questions that we want to address. We could attempt to answer them by focusing on forgiveness as a human experience apart from the influence of any faith commitments, but we will not take that tack. Instead we want to take the more difficult direction of illuminating forgiveness by exploring the connection between a faith perspective on it and the concrete human dynamics involved in it. This stance is itself a faith interpretation, but since the most objective science knows something about the necessity of taking a task-shaping perspective, we can take an explicit theological point of view without detracting from our results.

As we have implied, experiencing forgiveness causes the reassessment and the rearrangement of everything else in life. It includes a key revision in the way in which we think about God. God is not just a God of forgiveness but the ground of all reality and the power of the future. Putting forgiveness in the center marks God with personal loving features. Divine power serves love rather than being merely an exaltant power. Forgiveness elevates love of the most radical kind to ultimate dependability. It means that God can be trusted, making all the difference in the world.

Actually, forgiveness is a many-sided treasure in both theology and human relationships. I want to take a close look at this treasure and highlight at least seven of its essential features.

Forgiveness: An Asymmetrical Pattern

Forgiveness is not a neatly balanced relationship. It exalts the one who forgives to such an important place that dependence on that person shapes life differently. It builds community by letting things be unequal and open-ended. This very imbalance challenges any closure of the past and leaves room for a more promising future.

The asymmetrical pattern is created by the elevation of the

person who forgives. Forgiveness makes us dependent on an external initiative, not in a superficial way but in a way that presses us toward the permanent recognition of our dependence. Even in the most ordinary situation of forgiveness, there is a peculiar reliance on the initiative of the wronged person toward the other. Often it appears the other way around, as if the primary actor in the drama of forgiveness is the one who asks for it. After all one asks for forgiveness only when there is some confidence or hope that it might occur. In this sense, forgiveness seems to rest on the one who requests it. But on a deeper level it entails an assumption about the character of the wronged party. It is the willingness to forgive on the part of the one who has been wronged that makes forgiveness possible.

The importance of the forgiver is seen in instances where forgiveness is granted even when it is not sought. A person can forgive with or without a request for it. The forgiveness may not be effective in renewing the relationship until it is accepted, but the role of the forgiver still has priority in the transaction. Forgiveness always rests on an initiative that the guilty party cannot take alone.

This asymmetrical, unequal pattern in forgiveness makes forgiveness troubling. It is one reason why we prefer to deal with rights and the justification of behavior. Forgiveness puts us at the mercy of another. We cannot stand on our own integrity or performance. Forgiveness gives to the wronged one some kind of control over our future. No wonder forgiveness is often so difficult to take. Even a fair trade of "I'll forgive you for this, if you will forgive me for that" can be used to cover up the basic dynamics of forgiveness. A fair-trade mentality turns forgiveness into just another form of mutual self-justification.

In much of life we experience outside forces which press us to the wall, threatening us with such total control that our own identity seems endangered. We often balance these external forces by insisting on our own space for freedom. We learn to resist outside initiatives, and on many levels we must do just that in order to survive.

The attempt to turn away from forgiveness, and from the long-term dependence that it implies, may look like a victory. Closer examination, however, reveals cracks in the "Maginot Line" where defense is a sign of defeat. The sense of missed possibilities will not go away. Besides, forgiveness speaks to our fear of out-side control by introducing us to a special kind of external initia-tive. While the external initiative makes us dependent in some fundamental ways, it does not control us from the outside like so many other influences threaten to do. It speaks to our hearts and may win us over, but it is not sheer external pressure. It lifts our sights beyond efficient, mechanical causes to a matrix of per-sonal encounters where others can open doors for us without forcing us to walk through them. In this way, forgiveness lifts up an external initiative that introduces possibilities. It has the char-acter of invitation about it, going well beyond whatever can be predicted on the basis of the past.

Forgiveness brings a deeply personal perspective. It makes room for concern about fairness, even for the maximization of mathematical equity and comparable worth, but it does this against the background of a more fundamental affirmation of persons. The very possibility of forgiveness changes the charac-ter of reality, the shape and limits of human experience.

The key here is that someone needs to forgive, needs to go the second mile. If there is no one to do the forgiving, to pay the personal price, then we have to deal with problems in less per-sonal ways. We can start by trying to forgive ourselves without the benefit of another person's initiative, or we can pretend that forgiveness is a mistake, a kind of cheap way out. Certainly it is always tempting to make it work the old-fashioned way where everyone earns what they get. Finally, we can fashion fairness along a more equal distribution model and seem to avoid the need for mercy and forgiveness altogether.

While these approaches may be important on certain social and political levels, in the last analysis they can become the very mind-set that closes off deep and long-term personal commit-ments. Whenever life with others is dominated by a "contract" arrangement, both the individual and the individual's relation-ships with others are diminished.

What I want to note particularly is the way divine forgiveness sheds light on the reality of forgiveness in human affairs. Forgive-ness rests on an initiative from outside. We see this clearly in relation to God. The transaction is not between equals. By our-selves, we cannot make up for the sense of loss and guilt that comes from our decisions, our mistakes, or even our successes.

Before God, the very meaning of our lives depends on a power from beyond us that sustains, renews, and preserves. Forgiveness is a way of seeing that power in its most radically supportive role. We see that power in Jesus as the ultimate view of God's forgiveness. Against the unforgiving character of our time and circumstance, God's forgiveness in Christ makes us dependent on the initiative from another, an initiative that is dependable like no other source of resolution and restoration.

To grasp this theological truth is to return to the human scene with a new resolve not to absolutize any form of calculation as the ultimate path to wholeness. Rights are important, but they are not enough. No strict accounting will do. Understanding God's initiative leads us to look for situations where going beyond fairness is the answer. The forgiving initiative may be ours or another's, but the willingness to "hang a little loose" in relationships is precisely what forgiveness requires and what forgiveness brings into the picture. It builds community and relationship by letting things be unequal.

In the move beyond equality, what emerges is an affirmation of persons as special and particular. We do not all have the same role to play. We can be loved in our own particularity, even in our rebellion and weakness. Forgiveness is the opening for gracious affirmation, no matter what we have done. That is true between any two people, and it is also true in our relationship with God.

Forgiveness: Exalting the Ideal

Forgiveness takes ideals with great seriousness. It exalts the ideal as a judgment on reality. At the same time it turns failure into power and possibility. Forgiveness has a double thrust: It recognizes failure and then makes it a platform for a new assault on the future.

Forgiveness is not a relaxation of standards. On the contrary it upholds the ideal by a clear recognition that something has been lost, broken, or damaged. It actually elevates the ideal over against which guilt can be felt and forgiveness made relevant. Unless the standard holds, forgiveness simply makes no sense.

Forgiveness even has the capacity to enhance and to expand expectations. Instead of just reinforcing a past standard, forgiveness adds its own ingredient, a sort of yeast that stretches the materials that were there before. It raises the stakes in the whole business of assessing performance or fidelity. It makes the issues personal and deep beyond the mere breaking of rules or abstract ideals. The ideals take on the personal quality of one who cares enough to give in spite of rejection, failure, and pain. After forgiveness, then, a person does not stand in the same place as before. Expectations remain despite imperfection, but the horizon has shifted because of the personal factor introduced by forgiveness.

Forgiveness not only raises expectations but also sets free a new effort. New energies and commitment are born out of failure, for forgiveness frees us to mount an assault on the very challenges that led to defeat. Thus forgiveness turns failure into a new beginning. It takes yesterday's sense of loss and makes it power for tomorrow. This dual thrust is often evident in marital conflicts, or in other kinds of personal relationships, where a strange new potential for future action rises out of the ashes of defeat. So forgiveness is a priceless ingredient in human life. It stands against the two extremes of "anything goes" and "only perfection counts," and opens the door to a whole new approach to human affairs.

What is true in human interaction is also true in our relationship with God. Both of these aspects of life reflect the same double thrust of loss and gain. They tend to reinforce each other: The mystery of human forgiveness opens space for considering its divine manifestations, and the character of God's forgiveness invites application to human affairs.

In forgiveness our story is never finished. Before both our human companions and God, forgiveness adds a fresh dynamic to life. Ideals are enhanced and enlarged; but as they stretch before us forgiveness empowers us in surprising ways to make our problems the basis for new investments in one another and in the future.

Forgiveness: Facing Guilt

Forgiveness uses honesty to promote healing. It affirms that guilt is real but not the last word. It leads us into the reality of guilt, not so we will wallow in it in morbid and self-destructive ways but so we can find a genuine way beyond it. Forgiveness takes brokenness seriously. The process of forgiveness shows that guilt's consequences are painful and that some of the responsibility for its hurt rests squarely on our shoulders.

While forgiveness looks guilt in the eye and comes up with new beginnings, there are many forces in our society that insist that guilt is much better ignored or denied. In the film *The Unmarried Woman*, a troubled woman visits her psychiatrist. She talks about her feelings of guilt in a male/female relationship and indicates that she is profoundly affected by the feeling that she is contributing both to her own pain and to the suffering of another person. What she hears from the therapist is an appeal to deny the feelings of guilt and the reality that they would seem to reflect. She hears, "Your guilt isn't real."[1]

We can assume that the therapist intends to help this woman. Unfortunately, he seems to assume that the path to wholeness is followed by getting rid of the "fantasy" of guilt. If guilt can be denied or if it can be seen as an illusory attempt to blame oneself, then the woman's sense of responsibility might disappear and her self-image might improve.

An alternative therapeutic approach would deny guilt from the opposite direction. The guilt may be real, but it is not your guilt. You did the right thing; the problem is with someone else. Sometimes, of course, it is healthy to recognize that not all the guilt is ours, but a quick attempt to turn all the blame on others is not a real solution either. It can become its own kind of sickness—what M. Scott Peck likes to call a "character disorder."[2]

Forgiveness suggests that there is another, better way, which allows us to be honest about the reality of our own guilt and that of others. It encourages us to take honest responsibility for our side of the relationship. How much I contributed to the problem need not be determined precisely. What matters is the forthright acknowledgment that I was in the equation, and this acknowledgment can set the stage for the healing power of forgiveness.

Forgiveness transcends guilt, moving beyond behavior to our

1. See Robert N. Bellah et al., *Habits of the Heart* (Los Angeles: University of California Press, 1985), 47–48, for an interesting development of a one-sided approach to therapy where human problems are unduly simplified.

2. M. Scott Peck, *The Road Less Traveled* (New York: Simon and Schuster, 1978), 35.

very being. It asserts that care survives mistakes and rejections by establishing a relationship which is not destroyed by the failures that surface repeatedly in human life.

Forgiveness introduces a unique approach to healing, one that is both social and personal. It makes our self-image dependent on relationships, but not so dependent that initiatives cannot be taken. In any set of constraining circumstances, whether contrived by others or by us, there is something that we can do to move toward wholeness.

In this sense, forgiveness is a human tool for dealing with brokenness. A therapist can depend upon it; friends can appeal to it; lovers can remember their need for it. In the end, though, it is divine forgiveness that sets off a chain reaction in the whole range of human affairs. God's forgiveness provides a solid grounding for our initiatives. Honesty about guilt is not simply self-examination but a turn toward our Creator, before whom all responsibility must finally be assessed. Honesty before God finds a relationship in which forgiveness gives new power. The vision of life is changed. Guilt may speak with a loud voice, but forgiveness has the last word.

Forgiveness: Freedom for Relationships

Forgiveness is an initiative that liberates individuals without the loss of relationships. It asserts openness in the face of the momentum of past decisions; instead of isolating victims and oppressors, it opens the way to new beginnings.

Often when alienation and guilt have torn relationships apart, when people have felt victimized or have identified those who are guilty, efforts at restoring justice only increase the antagonism between the parties involved. Sometimes conformity to the letter of the law redresses certain inequities and avoids obvious oppressions, but this kind of justice may do little to build relationships. In fact, bondage to the letter of fairness can become a new kind of restriction that fails to promote relationships or to heal social situations.

When exact equality dominates without regard to the special situation and dignity of each person, the inertia of the calculations may yield something very different from the desired effect. The structures that create equal opportunity soon become the milieus of competition. The ensuing pain of winning and losing leaves those equalized in a profound kind of isolation. Robert N. Bellah claims that America's concern for the freedom of competition needed the counterbalance of certain values to moderate the often painful and isolating impact of unrestrained freedom.[3]

Forgiveness, or at least the recognition of its importance in certain situations, can function as one of these counterbalancing "habits of the heart." It picks up the need to temper the strict demands of justice with mercy. It maintains a climate in which there is another way to freedom besides the exact balancing of special interests. It offers a "habit" that complicates reality in marvelous ways, freeing people for relationships as interdependent persons who need one another in order to be and to become their "best" selves.

On certain levels of life, of course, strict concern for fairness and equity is absolutely essential. Laws are necessary and helpful. They promote a great amount of healthy freedom and mutual respect that does not depend on contingencies like the willingness to forgive. On these levels there are times when forgiveness is not the appropriate or immediate initiative.

Seeking freedom and justice without discerning the role of mercy and forgiveness has its own dangers. One of these is a vision of freedom and fairness that does not take into account the mutuality of human life. Leaving forgiveness out tempts us to see freedom as independence from the demands of another. While freedom is for the exercise of one's own will and activity, it should not diminish, or make superficial, our sense of mutual responsibility. If it does, the deep participation of humans in each other's lives can be missed.

Isolated, competitive freedom can parade under a concern for fairness, and fairness, if left to itself as a dominant concern, inevitably falls into a kind of mathematical analysis. It breaks relationships into independent factors that can be identified and numbered separately. In that analysis, the equality of integers may be preserved, but the cost is high. Interdependence and interaction can disappear. The interpersonal depth of what fairness was all about at its inception can be lost.

3. Bellah, et al., *Habits of the Heart*. Bellah follows Alexis de Tocqueville in a nineteenth-century interpretation of American culture.

When the concern is not just freedom from the pain of broken-ness but restoring the bond between human beings, the problem gets worse. Without attention to forgiveness, our attempts to put things back together only cause greater alienation. Continued focus on calculating proportionate responsibility and on protect-ing space for individual identities further isolates those pro-tected. It diminishes their reasons for celebrating shared reality.

Forgiveness, seen as possibility and power, opens a different route. Alienation, isolation, and competition for space can be bridged, diminished, and healed. What forgiveness brings to the quest for fairness is persistent commitments that can survive the unfairness of life. It brings a field of initiative into the picture that puts equality and fairness in their proper place. In the end, the kind of liberation forgiveness offers ties us together rather than separates us. It liberates by putting into the human situation the possibility of trust that goes deeper than fairness. It makes trust in another person possible in spite of the threat of unfairness and infidelity. It even takes the memory of injustice and turns it into only one factor for shaping the future. Forgiveness changes the entire situation for individuals. It frees them to be themselves—together. Sometimes this new situation will be reasonably fair, but forgiveness has the power to sustain identity even where equality is badly damaged or where it cannot be established in a completely satisfying way. Forgiveness can sustain the drive for greater fairness, but it does so precisely by going beyond it.

This agenda for liberation is different than self-assertion, dif-ferent than grand institutional programs for redressing struc-tural problems. It can work for individuals and groups. It is a vision of reality in which identities are real but never exactly equal. Chains of responsibility do not add up like an accountant's well-prepared balance sheet. Life together rests on a fabric of interdependence. The threads of our lives are woven so closely together that there is always a need for something from outside us. Forgiveness is the prime example of the ultimate kind of ini-tiative that is needed. Such an initiative is always precarious in human form, but that is what makes an understanding of God as forgiving so important. Interdependence finds its final ground in God and in the initiative of continuing love that generates forgive-ness at the very heart of things.

This power of forgiveness to change our situation is at work even on the most simple human level. A person who takes the initiative to forgive another demonstrates a truth that runs into the very depth of being. There is reality beyond the conflicts and fragmentation that set us against one another, and that reality can draw us forward together. It gives us things to do that make a difference in any set of circumstances. Jesus' saying, "Father, forgive them for they know not what they do" (Luke 23:34) is an example. Such forgiveness can be understood to apply even when those forgiven were fully aware of what they were doing. Such forgiveness restores on the deepest level, liberating us to be together and for one another.

Attention to the freedom created by forgiveness changes our situation. Even if we think of it as something only God can deal with, we stand in a new place. When the chips are down there is always another card to play and that option makes all the difference. Circumstances are never totally under our control, but there is an openness toward freedom in community ahead of us.

Forgiveness: Accepting Ambiguity

Forgiveness accepts things as they are without having to get everything sorted out, explained, or under control. It does not remove ambiguity with respect to the past and the future. Instead it works in the middle of this abiding ambiguity, giving us a place to stand on our journey through life.

As we move from the past, we are tempted to find out exactly who was responsible for what. We want to pinpoint guilt and innocence with such clarity that present actions and consequences can flow directly from this assessment. We produce a kind of bondage to the past. In contrast, forgiveness allows the past to remain unsettled. The willingness to forgive makes careful and complete analysis of all that has happened less important than it might otherwise be. Some things can be left hidden from view. When the offended party can forgive whatever the guilt might be, absolute clarity about "who did what to whom" is not crucial.

In part, acceptance of the past without final explanations comes because forgiveness focuses more on persons than on isolated behavior. It is persons who are forgiven, not merely deeds or omissions. Specifying some behavior that makes forgiveness relevant may be important, but the energy of forgiving moves quickly toward the person who is forgiven, pushing the entire enumeration of detailed behavior into secondary or even trivial importance.

I am reminded of Martin Luther's criticism of the medieval penitential system where strict recital of all past sins to the priest or to God did not seem to get at the deepest problem of all—the broken personal relationship. Forgiveness, taken superficially, seems to be hung up on mistakes, specific injuries, and associated guilt; but if forgiveness is followed to its depths it puts the relationship between persons into the foreground. We may need to start with something specific, but if we stop there we close off the power of forgiveness.

Leaving the past alone is to turn away from self-justification and wounded retribution. In this way, forgiveness gives freedom from the past and from its pain. Something more promising captures our attention. The wonder of a person who can forgive puts our eyes on present and future interactions with that person. There is tremendous potential for gain in being willing to let the past retain some of its unexplored ambiguity.

Forgiveness adds a different dimension to the frequent concern in psychotherapy to pursue self-examination to its limits. It is a resource that moves us beyond a persistence in looking at the past. It gives pastoral counseling a different look than much of secular psychotherapy. The difference is not just religious language or ecclesiastical connections but a different prescription for dealing with our own history.

Forgiveness retains a second type of ambiguity—the ambiguity concerning the future. It entails a respect for people that leaves them free of clear-cut contracts about the future. It liberates them from expecting perfect results or a perfect resolution, even when a new beginning has been established.

Forgiveness is not a way of controlling the other person, so it also frees us from expecting the future to be without new challenges, new disappointments, new occasions in which forgiveness will have to do its work. A certain openness to the future, a risk of loss or gain, remains and must be left open precisely because the future is built on a different vision. Just as forgiveness accepts ambiguity in the past, so it does not seek to resolve all future conflicts ahead of time. It "hangs loose" to the results of its own achievements.

All of this makes forgiveness an ingredient in human affairs that can accept ambiguity and openness, not as unfinished business but as the very framework of life's adventure in partnership with others. This ambiguity leaves room for shaping the future together. We are left free, even when the cost is more pain and the need for further forgiveness will occur again.

Forgiveness: Suffering for Others

Forgiveness arises out of pain and adds painful features of its own. It hurts to forgive as the pain of the past is taken on willingly by the innocent party. Forgiveness involves suffering for others, but it can also hurt to have to be forgiven.

In broken relationships, people suffer because of wrong done to them and by them. Facing up to the suffering that I have caused is one thing, but being willing to take the suffering caused by another person without requiring the last "pound of flesh" is a very different story. The acceptance of suffering for the sake of another person is an essential ingredient in forgiveness. We take the burden from another and share the load. It can be called "vicarious suffering" where the one who forgives represents and receives another person's due. There can be no forgiveness without the willingness of persons to take pain upon themselves, sometimes at a great price.

At this point, it is important to note the difference between vicarious suffering and other kinds of unhelpful suffering. The suffering involved in honest forgiveness is not masochistic suffering for its own sake. Sometimes suffering arises from a lack of self-worth. The forgiver strains to carry a calculus of guilt under the facade of forgiveness. Suffering for another may be taken on because persons feel that they really deserve it. The suffering involved in forgiveness cannot be reduced to that motive. In forgiveness, the initiative to share the pain of the other person is a positive, life-affirming venture. It accepts suffering that is undeserved as the best way to move on.

In a similar way, vicarious suffering can be construed as a way of controlling another person. Doing it *for* them turns out to be doing it *to* them. The person pays the price but never lets the offender forget it. The object of the suffering is not to renew the friendship but to reassert a kind of dominance that may have been part of the original problem.

In contrast, real forgiveness accepts vicarious suffering as an unavoidable by-product of concern and respect for the other person. It is not suffering sought for its own sake or as a means of asserting power. It is suffering that is taken on as the price of a hopeful future. We can speak of forgiveness, and of the suffering it entails, as love's leverage against the past. Against the tendency to see the past as totally determining the future, forgiveness opens the past and its consequences to new possibilities. If another person takes some of the undeserved pain upon his or her shoulders, the past cannot control the outcome, leaving the future more open. This is what forgiveness is all about. When forgiveness is mutual its power to open up new possibilities is clearest, but the risk of reducing either side to an equity relationship is also greatest. Suffering for the sake of the other, though, makes the grand mystery of forgiveness stand out with clarity. When a person is willing to do that, the future is promising.

God's forgiveness and his willingness to pay the price of that forgiveness make a real difference in our vision of human life. If God is seen as pure justice or strict retribution, we look to the future as a mechanical, deterministic playing out of consequences made inevitable by events in the past. In contrast, if God is seen as the One who again and again shoulders the world's burdens for the sake of others, our entire cosmic and future expectations take a different shape. A suffering God, a forgiving God provides a basis for expecting genuinely fresh opportunities, possibilities for renewal and restoration. The future is not just a series of predetermined consequences. It is a place where the trajectories of individuals and events can be changed. The healing, hopeful power of suffering love will have to be taken into account. This is no mechanical, impersonal world, but a place where purpose and will always make a difference. When promises of an abiding, suffering love are there, life has a different flavor with respect to God and in the diverse interactions that we have with one another.

Forgiveness, then, can be seen as shaping a very different vision of reality, precisely because of its emphasis on unmerited suffering. Vicarious suffering is no dead end. It is not wallowing in pain because we have to. It opens the future as both the completion and the correction of the past. Forgiveness enriches the future with genuinely new possibilities, opportunities that we had no right to expect. When forgiveness is in the picture, all of life has wondrous potential for change, for growth, for renewal.

Forgiveness: Space for a Personal God

Forgiveness opens space for a personal God who takes free, restoring initiatives. God as the ground and goal of all human endeavor is not some rigid reality that we simply bump up against. God is not a kind of impersonal law maker or an objective judge who stands at a distance from human affairs. Stressing forgiveness makes God, as ultimate context, a personal and caring reality in whom human life has place and meaning. God has a unique role to play in relation to each one of us and contributes to every kind of partnership that emerges in the human situation.

The God who wills to forgive is personal. This does not reduce God's reality to persons as we know them, but it does mean, as Paul Tillich says, that God is not less than personal. That means that God has some kind of life and consciousness like our own. God has purposes, concerns, satisfactions, and even the capacity to suffer. There is a divine ability to respond to every situation in its particularity. That is what persons amount to—actors in the drama of history who initiate, respond, experience, and remember. God, as ultimate forgiver, is personal. To trust in that forgiving God changes our entire approach to relationships.

A personal God makes a difference on the human level; the special character of human individuals and circumstances is enhanced. There are no general rules for behavior, no patterns that must be affirmed as the unqualified standard for human relationships. Instead in every circumstance, in every person's life, in every conflict-ridden encounter, there is space for the peculiar intervention of forgiveness and love.

Forgiveness means that wholeness is never merely conformity to some external or universal standard. Wholeness is found in recognizing the special circumstances, the special needs, even the unheard-of offenses that seem like they can never be overcome. Forgiveness transforms these specific features of the human problem into new opportunities.

In the midst of it all, persons who need to be forgiven are treated as being worth the price. They are cared for beyond anything that can be justified; they are loved in spite of what they are or what they do. This forgiving love transforms the reality of the one who is loved. It opens the door to new possibilities, to new self-images, to restored relationships, to transformed behavior.

This new life happens when humans forgive. When God is seen as the forgiving One, a broader horizon is offered. Our perspective is deepened. God's forgiveness introduces new strength for our forgiving initiatives. It transforms our failures in the long-term perspective so that we can forgive again. It keeps us from giving up on the specialness of people and the unique needs of particular situations. It makes pastoral counseling, the consolation between Christian brothers and sisters, powerful. Pastoral counseling is not just the office or the professional skill of the pastor. It is not just the care of another person. It means that our attempts to love and forgive rest on the reality of our being loved and forgiven by God and that puts life in new perspective and opens up a whole new horizon.

If the dynamics of forgiveness on a human level prompt us to look to God, the whole history of God in Christ presses toward center stage. In Christ, forgiveness is made clear. The deep, personal dimensions of freedom in relationships surface. God is seen as the lover who suffers for the guilty in such a dependable and decisive way that we can build all our hope around him.

Conclusion

I have tried to walk the bridge between human forgiveness and divine reality. I hope that I have helped us to see the power of God's forgiveness breaking into our world and impinging on our lives. Perhaps I have also shed light on the dynamics of counseling and care, especially in its pastoral and Christian modes.

As travelers on life's way, we often look for someone to tell us that we are right in our decisions and behavior. We fight to justify ourselves and look to find someone to verify our status. Forgiveness offers another route. It takes guilt and loss seriously and opens up the future to new possibilities. Even if only one person forgives another, the power of change is far greater than all attempts at self-justification and mutual admiration. By taking loss or guilt seriously, forgiveness shares in the suffering of the other person, making risk bearable and the future hopeful.

When this forgiveness is God forgiving, the freshness of the future has cosmic ground and eternal dependability. "Your sins are forgiven. . . . Take up your bed and go home" (Matt. 9:2, 6). Forgiveness in this sense is new life. It recasts human failure into a new beginning and finite hope into recreated relationships.

14

Forgiveness and the Healing of the Family

RINDA G. ROGERS

For several decades psychotherapists have dealt with a frustrating phenomenon: Gains made by clients in the course of individual psychotherapy are often compromised when these clients return to their families. Powerful forces within the family act together to force the client back to former ways of relating. Indeed, the very family who asks the therapist to help the dysfunctional member often ends up resisting the behavioral and attitudinal changes that take place within the client. The family, heavily invested in old ways of living, may put intense pressure on the client, especially if he or she broke the family rule that says, "Asking for help is a sign of weakness. We make it on our own."

Sooner or later, though, the client must return to the family for the perilous task of trying to be part of a dialogue in which relationships are reworked. Ideally, there should be safety and fairness for each member in the family system. The wholeness of the family, and the individuation of each of its members, should not be purchased at the cost of any individual within the system.

Instead the family should provide its members with a balanced opportunity for both individuation and interrelationship.[1]

To live up to this potential the family must be healed of its tendency to resist the individuating member. I want to address and, I hope, to elucidate this issue. More specifically, I want to explore the role of forgiveness in family systems and try to highlight the way in which it is a healing force in broken or stagnant relationships.

My understanding of the family is based on the contextual school of family system analysis as elaborated by Ivan Borzymeny-Nagy, Margaret Cotroneo, and others.[2] Within this framework, I will start by setting forth the contextual understanding of the basic way in which families are distorted or stagnant. Then I will turn to a contextual understanding of forgiveness as part of the process by which families are healed. Finally, I will draw implications from our study, considering forgiveness in the family in the context of the church.

A Contextual Understanding of the Problem

The contextual approach to family systems relies heavily on the notion of reciprocity in relationships. Reciprocity, or mutuality, represents a balance between obligations and entitlements, that is, between what a person "owes" others in the system and what others "owe" him or her. A proper balance between these two is seldom achieved. In fact, in most families members feel cheated in one way or another, believing that they have not given or received what is justly due. "Relational accounts" within the family are then said to be unbalanced, and the family system usually gets stuck, or turns stagnant, in that condition.

Members who are cut off, literally or metaphorically, from the family have been removed from the human story which began before them and which continues after them. They no longer ex-

1. Individuation should not be confused with individualism or "me-ism." It is not the self-centered pursuit of one's own thing but the genuine growth of oneself in the context of others.

2. Ivan Boszormenyi-Nagy and Geraldine M. Spark, *Invisible Loyalties: Reciprocity in Intergenerational Therapy* (Hagerstown, Md.: Harper and Row, 1973); Margaret Cotroneo, "Forgiveness Is an Act of Relationship," *Campus Ministry Report* 4, United States Catholic Conference, N.D., 4.

perience themselves as being a part of that story, with its web of roles, its multigenerational transmission of family experiences, its accrued deposit of wisdom, lore, and values. There is no one present to them to remind them of who they are and of how they fit into the ongoing story. This vacuum often sets them off in search of something that will fill the void. Some people get stuck permanently in the fruitless attempt to repair the damage.

In this analysis of family life two concepts, really two dynamics, are especially important—loyalty and trust. Loyalty refers to the keeping of family rules regarding the way entitlements and obligations are discharged. The exercise of loyalty in the family is healthy and productive; the absence of it is detrimental to all concerned. But if the family considers growing up and becoming independent a betrayal or a disloyalty, then the individual members may suffer as they attempt to individuate, even though they may try to do so within the context of interrelationships.

Trust is the single most bankable currency in human reciprocal relationships. It is being dependable and faithful in the discharge of loyalty or, more holistically, it is being there for another person. Reserves of trust are built up in the family when its members provide reliable, dependable care for one another with little exploitation, that is, with as little using of the other as possible. Reserves of mistrust can also be built up, such as in children who have not had their basic needs satisfied regularly or in the young adult who is harassed into becoming a physician in order to fulfill his or her father's unmet ambition.

The contextual therapist is interested in how loyalty and trust have been exercised in the generational history of the family. Have obligations been met and entitlements been received in a way that is fair or just to all members? What wounds have been created by unbalanced relationships? More specifically, what deficit of reliable parental care has been suffered by the child? How has this deficit expressed or repeated itself in one form or another throughout the family's history? These questions are related to the family's legacy, or to its inheritance, and they deal with relational dynamics that may be passed on from generation to generation.

Murray Bowen identified the modus operandi of exploitation

when he clarified the operation of triangulation in families.[3] Edwin H. Friedman says, "An emotional triangle is formed by any three persons or issues. . . . The basic law of emotional triangles is that when any two parts of a system become uncomfortable with one another, they will 'triangle in' or focus upon a third person, or issue, as a way of stabilizing their own relationship with one another."[4] Friedman goes on to indicate that people may be drawn into triangles, or they may actually triangulate themselves into an unstable or exploitative relationship. In any case, they tend to stabilize, at least temporarily, a relationship that should be reexamined or reworked. A concrete example will help to clarify the point.

Pastor Tee, who became a minister at his mother's insistence, accepts money from her so he can live beyond his means and can impress his wealthy congregation. He exploits his mother's need to live through him, even though he resents her constant interference in his affairs and her assumption that she can make certain claims on his time and position. When Pastor Tee has had enough, he complains to his wife and expects her to deal with his mother. The mother, in turn, becomes upset with her son's attitude and looks to the wife as an ally against him.

As both pastor and mother dump anguish on the wife, triangulation occurs and, in the process, the wife suffers from stress hypertension. The wife should be advised to "detriangulate," that is, to refuse to take sides with either mother or son and to refer them back to each other. This step, of course, would be very difficult for her to take, partly because triangulation tends to operate unconsciously and partly because both pastor and mother would immediately question her loyalty and trust. Nevertheless, the wife should refuse to serve as intermediate host of any loaded communication between them. In a justice-delivering family system, accounts would be balanced between entitlements and obligations, and there would be a minimum of exploitation with care giving.

This contextual analysis of distorted family dynamics can be put in a theological framework. With God we are never exploited,

3. Murray Bowen, *Family Therapy in Clinical Practice* (New York: Aronson, 1978).

4. Edwin H. Friedman, *Generation to Generation: Family Process in Church and Synagogue* (New York: Guilford, 1985), 20.

for his care is prevenient, consistent, and trustworthy. He initiates and sustains relationship with us and fulfills the entitlements given to us at birth, partly in and through the church (initially in baptism) and partly in the family when it acts as his creative agent by helping us to become who we are. God also calls us to the larger task of providing trustworthy care to others. Our fallen state, though, means that, despite his incarnation in our hearts, we have a tendency to use others for our own ends. When we exploit others we rob them of their birthright and contribute to the breakdown of the family into isolated and even warring components.

Individualism not only fractures the family but also threatens the integration and individuation of the very self that is at the core of the *imago Dei*. The phenomenon of the soul turned inward upon itself has dogged us since the fall. This fragmenting deification of the self is well entrenched in our culture and can be easily encouraged by a family where there is little or no reciprocity.

A Contextual Understanding of Forgiveness

The contextual understanding of forgiveness rests on the notion of what is called multipartiality. In any dialogue of repair and maintenance all sides must be heard and given genuine credence. This notion assumes that in the family everyone has a "side," a version of what it has been like to be in the system. Inevitably, no two family members experience the family in the same way. When any person's side, therefore, is absent or sacrificed by its underentitled owner or discounted by its overentitled listener, the truth of the whole system is not represented, and relationships within the system become brittle and superficial. Individuals must protect themselves from the unheard story, so there is little genuine trust among them.

Multipartiality means, Margaret Cotroneo suggests, that forgiveness is an act of relationship. In fact, it means that the burden of forgiveness no longer rests on only one member of the family; it is, or should be, seated in the family system itself. Thus forgiveness carries with it both entitlements and obligations for everyone in the system.

According to Cotroneo, forgiveness is a multiphased act or process. First, it is a "turning," specifically a turning toward oneself to acknowledge not only one's own role in the family's damaged relationships but also one's own sense of being damaged or even abandoned by the family. One's perceptions must be communicated to other members of the family in an appropriate way, whether they are able to hear it or not at the time. In any case,

> by facing and examining one's own perceptions of a broken relationship, an initiating act of giving is done, which starts to rebalance a stagnant and unsatisfactory balance of giving and receiving. Freed from a frozen position of unilateral lack of forgiveness and of scapegoating, a person who is finally able to turn and face his (her) part in an injured relationship, experiences the beginning of genuine liberation.[5]

Cotroneo reminds us that this act of self-giving is more significant than its immediate outcome. Indeed, she says, the result may be "apparent rejection and continued intransigency on the part of the other." In spite of this possible outcome, Cotroneo maintains that healing has begun to occur, because someone has taken the first step to renew "the possibilities for rebalancing the ledger of exploitative and unjust relatedness."[6]

The second phase is called "facing" or, more fully, "facing reciprocal indebtedness." It refers to hearing the other's story, either through the imagination if the person is not available or through actual listening if contact can be made. The goal is to come to an appreciation of how this person is bound to the family ledger and how he or she was affected by it. If the person is not available because of death or distance, learning the details of the person's history in the family can be a helpful substitute for actual encounter. Most families have an oral tradition in which some significant information is embedded.

For Cotroneo facing reciprocal indebtedness requires more of the listener than simply the good intention to hear. It requires a serious consideration of the consequences inflicted by an injury and concrete steps to repair the damage. Good intentions without action are not sufficient. In fact, they may be self-serving and therefore exploitative, contributing to the distance between the injured party and the one who has done the injury. "Injured persons are entitled to have their injuries rebalanced through free

5. Margaret Cotroneo, "Forgiveness."
6. Ibid.

giving of the guilty (exploiting) party. Only then is an injured person free to cooperate in healing the relationship."[7]

Finally, forgiveness includes "reclaiming," that is, identifying and owning past and present resources in the relationship. It involves the acceptance of one's legacy by acknowledging what one has given and received in the history of the family. Anamnesis helps with the recall of what existed between the participants in the past, including the invisible loyalties that bound the family together for better or worse.

This threefold act of forgiveness can be illuminated by applying it to Pastor Tee and his mother. Because Pastor Tee has not been faced with his mother's story, he does not know what possible deficits there are in her family-of-origin and family-of-marriage ledgers that she may be trying to recalibrate by her controlling, solicitous behavior toward him. In all likelihood, she is not aware of her own ledger issues as they exist in the relationship with her son. Furthermore, she has probably not heard her son's ledger issues, specifically his need for, and his entitlement to, her unconditional love. He may feel heavily indebted to her for the help she has given him, but she may be unaware of it because he has never told her or because she may not trust what he is saying. In any case, she feels rejected when he accepts her money but rebuffs her many other attempts to be helpful. To begin to repair this relationship three activities must take place.

First, in terms of "turning" each person needs to acknowledge his or her own role in the stagnant relationship. Both individuals must see how they are using each other to meet unfulfilled expectations. They must see that these expectations are probably driven by deficits incurred in earlier generations and that they persist because they have never been recalibrated. Mother and son will begin to appreciate how the "sins of the fathers and mothers" surface anew in each generation, binding them together in a stagnant, unjust relationship that is not satisfying to either one of them. The process of forgiveness will begin as they recognize that the issue is not blame but boundness to the family ledger. They will take their first step toward each other.

In the "facing" phase, Pastor Tee and his mother must come to know of each other's feelings of guilt for the deficits that have not

7. Ibid.

been corrected. In a more positive vein a specific account of each other's care and consideration for the other needs to be acknowledged and can begin to offset the perpetuated deficits. The identified positives are more than a history of past trust between the two of them. They are resources for continued relationship in which new trust-building takes place.

In the third phase, Pastor Tee and his mother must weigh together the potential for "reclaiming" their relationship. Other members of the family may have to be included in the rebalancing, for they are a vital part of the drama. The lack of trust that has existed between mother and son has affected all of them. The pastor's wife has had high blood pressure, and no doubt the children have been triangulated by the adult members of the family. As trust grows between pastor and mother, the need for triangulation can be expected to diminish.

We need to admit that the present stalemate between Pastor Tee and his mother may not be healed in the foreseeable future. Too many deficits, too many moments of hurtful injustice may have transpired in the relationship. Nevertheless, both mother and son are obligated to hear each other on account of their membership in a shared story. They may first have to come to know their own ledger, their own story, but certainly they need to attend to each other's ledger in terms of obligations and entitlements. By working together to balance and repair certain identified deficits, trust will begin to grow between them. By looking at elements in their relationship that have worked for them in the past, they will begin to rebalance the multigenerational ledger that will become a legacy to their children.

Forgiveness as an act of relationship is a way of continually addressing and restoring the balance of accounts in a family system. It is a way of recalibrating wounds sustained within the family as a result of a deficit of caring vis-à-vis one's entitlements. It is not a one-sided activity of writing off someone's failure to live up to relational obligations, but it is a dialogical activity that requires conversation in which all members of the family participate.

Forgiveness is crucial to the healing of the family, to its processes and its members. In the absence of forgiveness, the family tends to fragment and its members tend to pursue their own destinies independent of God and of one another. Some families may collapse altogether. But in the presence of forgiveness, families tend to fulfill their God-appointed design. Forgiveness encourages a relationship for each family member that is balanced between mutual association and individual differentiation. It establishes an I-Thou context in which trust and justice flourish.

Forgiveness and the Church

The stages of forgiveness that Cotroneo has identified suggest that it is advantageous to have a systems-wise third party who will function as objective prophet and guide. The customary term for such a person is "therapist," but one could call him or her a "family process confessor."

There is theological support for this notion. "Turning" and "facing," as laid out in Cotroneo's contextual system, bears striking similarity to confession and repentance. The disclosure of one's injury and injuring applies to the psalmist's words that are used in the Lutheran order for "Individual Confession and Forgiveness."[8]

> O Lord, open my lips, and my mouth shall
>   declare your praise.
> Had you desired it, I would have offered sacrifice,
>   but you take no delight in burnt offerings.
> The sacrifice of God is a troubled spirit;
>   a broken and contrite heart, O God, you
>   will not despise.
> Have mercy on me, O God, according to your
>   lovingkindness; in your great compassion
>   blot out my offenses.
> Wash me through and through from my wickedness,
>   and cleanse me from my sin. (Ps. 51:15–17, 1–2)

The Lutheran order goes on to invite the penitent to confess specific sins, that is, to identify and own up to one's particular role in the troubles at hand. And when the rubrics call for a "pastoral conversation" they present the opportunity to look precisely

---

8. Association of Evangelical Lutheran Churches et al., *Occasional Services: A Companion to Lutheran Book of Worship* (Minneapolis: Augsburg; Philadelphia: Board of Publications, Lutheran Church in America), 45.

at what is written on the family ledger and to determine the balance of accounts receivable (entitlements) and accounts payable (obligations).

It would not be difficult to build upon the rite of confession in such a way as to invite the whole family to take part in it. In this way the family could begin to learn to mediate forgiveness, moving through confession and into what becomes absolution in the forgiveness process. When the family comes to the reclamation phase a review is made of all the positive resources that exist in relationship to each other. This balancing action is good stewardship, and it tends to activate resources that are overlooked in the heat of struggle.

For a few families this process will result in the realization that there are insufficient resources within the system for it to go on in its present form. The audit of relational accounts shows that the positive resources created in trust by the meeting of entitlements and the discharging of obligations are overwhelmed by injury and trauma. For example, child abuse, war trauma, and drug and alcohol dependency can all seriously compromise a family's ability to continue to provide for its members. Ideally, it would be at this point that the confessor would absolve the family on the grounds that the process had been faithfully applied, that every relational stone had been turned over, and that it was time to withdraw further investment in a system that cannot deliver fairly to its members. Those in the church who have sought to minister to divorced individuals may be on the right track in the sense of trying to help the participants make closure and thus cease from wounding one another.

Whatever the future of any given family unit, the process of forgiveness as identified by Cotroneo offers the family an opportunity to function as the body of Christ, mediating forgiveness through the systemic confessional process and its relational, reclaiming activity. In any case, the family system, with its own dynamic character, is every bit as *simul iustus et peccator* as the individuals who belong to it. If true, then forgiveness must finally be a family affair, or when it is engaged in individually it must result in a return to the family for its completion.

God has ordained an identity-bearing function for the family, but the family invariably gets wounded and unbalanced in its ledger accounts. Identity suffers or is distorted, and forgiveness is a daily necessity. This forgiveness, this return to the family via confession and renewal is nothing less than a return to baptism, reclaiming our God-given identity.

I would like to think that the family could be trained over time to exercise the activity of forgiveness on a daily basis. The techniques of trust-building offer a possibility. For example, families could be encouraged and taught to share personal histories cross-generationally as they look at old albums and view home movies together. Individual family members could be invited to log their perception of the family's "Ten Commandments." Sharing these perceptions would be a way to begin to hear each other's "side."

The parish church is the place where these things must be fostered. Parishes can assist with the design, support, and delivery of the process of family confession. They have a distance to go before developing an intentional ministry that does not preach at families but teaches them. In the meantime, the church's individual order for confession and forgiveness should be adapted to include Cotroneo's process of turning, facing, and reclaiming. Then forgiveness becomes an act of relationship. It becomes a return to the family which, in actuality, is a healing of its injuries and a fulfillment of its potential.

Conclusion

As people of God, we share in an ultimate story and are members of a cosmic family. When we read biblical lessons aloud every Sunday, we are telling those stories to each other and to our children. We seldom articulate the connection between these stories and the stories of our own families. We are not being explicit about how God calls our family life into being and shapes its destiny. We ignore our accountability to him and to each other, and individualize his presence and work among us. Forgiveness as an act of relationship offers us another possibility. It heals the family covenants that have been broken and makes us into a community of entitled and obligated people. It empowers us to move toward what we essentially are—persons within a community of persons.[9]

9. See Paul Tillich, *Morality and Beyond* (New York: Harper, 1963), 19.

Conclusion

David G. Benner

The preceding chapters give ample evidence of the essential nature of the human predicament. As a result of sin (this being variously viewed in these chapters as mismanagement of anxiety, rebellion, moral turpitude, idolatrous choices in the search for comfort and security, and pride) humans find themselves alienated from God, themselves, and others. One of the major psychospiritual consequences of this state of alienation is the experience of guilt; the discussion of the dynamics of guilt has, therefore, been a central part of our focus.

But if this book were only to focus on the human plight and fail to point to the hope for our rescue it would not be faithful to the Christian gospel. The gospel always meets us where we are and does so in a way that provides us with a penetrating analysis of our predicament. However, it would never have been called "gospel" or "good news" if it left us with this now sharpened understanding of our plight but failed to identify the means for our healing. That healing is found in the extravagant grace of a forgiving God who comes to us, seeking us out and pursuing us even as we flee him, and brings us the healing which we so desperately need.

Forgiveness is central to this process of healing. This is not merely a superficial overlooking of our sin or a rearranging of a divine ledger, for that would never be radical enough to remedy the sickness with which we are infected. Rather it is a restoration of a relationship. Now back in right relationship with God we have the hope of discovering our true selves and of being able to live at peace with what we find. We also have the hope of discovering others, meeting them in nonexploitative intimacy instead of self-serving manipulation.

This is the God who comes to us "with healing in his wings." And in his name so we also come to those whom we encounter in the healing ministries. Forgiveness is once again central in these relationships. It is not merely our forgiveness of those with whom we work, but much more profoundly, our pointing them toward the possibility and ultimate source of forgiveness.

These related foci of sin, guilt, and forgiveness form one of the most fertile intersections of psychology and theology. Our understanding of the dynamics of both the human predicament and hope for healing are greatly enhanced as we allow psychology and theology to interact.

Because of the central place these questions play in the human situation, this book represents neither the first nor the last word on the subject. In fact, it is obvious that much remains to be worked out. This is particularly true with regard to forgiveness. Why does it so often seem impossible to forgive another person or even oneself? How does the counselor or therapist help someone move toward forgiveness? How can children learn to forgive their parents, and parents, their children? And how can we make forgiveness more regularly a part of our life together in Christian community? These are but a few of the important questions that require further work as we move toward incorporating the insights contained within this volume into our lives and relationships.

We began this book by stating that an understanding of sin, guilt and the need for forgiveness must be a part of any adequate understanding of the human predicament. So the same understanding must lie at the heart of our therapeutic efforts. Healers must be those who know their own sinfulness, who can make a constructive, rather than a neurotic and retroflective, response to their guilt, and who have known the liberation that accompanies both the receiving and giving of forgiveness. It is hoped that this book has made a contribution to this end.

Bibliography

Aden, LeRoy. "Faith and the Developmental Cycle." *Pastoral Psychology* 24 (Spring 1976): 215–30.

———. "On Carl Rogers' Becoming." *Theology Today* 36, 4 (Jan. 1980): 556–59.

Aden, LeRoy, and J. Harold Ellens, eds. *The Church and Pastoral Care.* Grand Rapids: Baker, 1988.

Allport, Gordon W. *The Individual and His Religion.* New York: Macmillan, 1950.

Angyal, Andras. "The Convergence of Psychotherapy and Religion." *Journal of Pastoral Care* 5, 4 (1951): 4–14.

———. *Neurosis and Treatment: A Holistic Theory.* New York: John Wiley and Sons, 1965.

———. "A Theoretical Model for Personality Studies." *Journal of Personality* 20, 1 (1951): 132.

Arnold, William. *Introduction to Pastoral Care.* Philadelphia: Westminster, 1982.

Becker, Arthur. *Guilt: Curse or Blessing?* Minneapolis: Augsburg, 1977.

Becker, Ernest. *The Denial of Death.* New York: Free, 1973.

———. *Escape from Evil.* New York: Free, 1975.

Belgum, David. *Guilt: Where Psychology and Religion Meet.* Englewood Cliffs, N.J.: Prentice-Hall, 1963.

Bellah, Robert N., et al. *Habits of the Heart.* Los Angeles: University of California Press, 1985.

Berry, C. Markham. "Entering Canaan: Adolescence as a Stage of Spiritual Growth." *Bulletin* 6, 4 (1980): 10–13.

Boisen, Anton. *Explorations of the Inner World.* New York: Harper and Brothers, 1936.

———. *Out of the Depths.* New York: Harper and Row, 1960.

_____. "Religious Experience and Psychological Conflict." *American Psychologist* 13 (1958): 568–70.

Bonhoeffer, Dietrich. *The Cost of Discipleship*. Trans. Reginald H. Fuller. New York: Macmillan, 1948.

_____. *Ethics*. Ed. Eberhard Bethge, trans. Neville H. Smith. New York: Macmillan, 1955.

_____. *Letters and Papers from Prison*. Trans. Reginald H. Fuller. New York: Macmillan, 1953.

Boss, Medard. *Psychoanalysis and Daseinanalysis*. New York: Basic, 1963.

Boszormenyi-Nagy, Ivan, and Geraldine M. Spark. *Invisible Loyalties: Reciprocity in Intergenerational Therapy*. Hagerstown, Md.: Harper, 1973.

Bowen, Murray. *Family Therapy in Clinical Practice*. New York: Aronson, 1978.

Brecht, Martin. *Martin Luther: His Road to Reformation*. Trans. John L. Schaaf. Philadelphia: Fortress, 1985.

Browning, Don S. "A Doctrine of the Atonement Informed by the Psychotherapeutic Process." *Journal of Pastoral Care* 17 (1963): 136–47.

_____. *The Moral Context of Pastoral Care*. Philadelphia: Westminster, 1976.

_____. *Religious Ethics and Pastoral Care*. Philadelphia: Fortress, 1983.

Brueggemann, Walter. "Covenanting as Human Vocation." *Interpretation* 33 (April 1979): 115–29.

Buber, Martin. "Guilt and Guilt Feelings." *Psychiatry* 20 (1957): 117–50.

_____. *I and Thou*. New York: Scribners, 1958.

Campbell, Alastair V. *Rediscovering Pastoral Care*. Philadelphia: Westminster, 1981.

Capps, Donald. *Life Cycle Theory and Pastoral Care*. Philadelphia: Fortress, 1983.

_____. *Pastoral Care and Hermeneutics*. Philadelphia: Fortress, 1984.

Clebsch, William A., and Charles R. Jaekle. *Pastoral Care in Historical Perspective*. Englewood Cliffs, N.J.: Prentice-Hall, 1964.

Clinebell, Howard, Jr. *Basic Types of Pastoral Care and Counseling*. 2d ed. Nashville: Abingdon, 1984.

_____. *Understanding and Counseling the Alcoholic Through Religion and Psychology*. Nashville: Abingdon, 1956.

Collins, Gary. *Search for Reality*. Wheaton, Ill.: Key, 1969.

Cotroneo, Margaret. "Forgiveness Is an Act of Relationship." *Campus Ministry Report* 4, 4.

Daim, Wilfred. *Depth Psychology and Salvation*. New York: Unger, 1963.

Ellens, J. Harold. "Biblical Themes in Psychological Theory and Practice." *Bulletin* 6, 2 (1980): 2–6.

_____. *God's Grace and Human Health*. Nashville: Abingdon, 1982.

Emerson, James G. *The Dynamics of Forgiveness*. Philadelphia: Westminster, 1964.

Erikson, Erik H. *Identity and the Life Cycle*. New York: International Universities Press, 1959.

————. *Insight and Responsibility*. New York: Norton, 1964.

Flugel, J. C. *Man, Morals, and Society*. New York: Viking, 1961.

Forde, Gerhard. *The Law-Gospel Debate*. Minneapolis: Augsburg, 1969.

Frankl, Viktor E. *Man's Search for Meaning: An Introduction to Logotherapy*. Boston: Beacon, 1962.

Friedman, Edwin H. *Generation to Generation: Family Process in Church and Synagogue*. New York: Guilford, 1985.

Freud, Sigmund. *Autobiography*. New York: W. W. Norton, 1935.

————. *Civilization and Its Discontents*. Trans. Joan Riviere. London: Hogarth, 1969.

————. *The Ego and the Id*. Trans. Joan Riviere. London: Hogarth, 1927.

————. *New Introductory Lectures in Psychoanalysis*. Trans. W. J. H. Sprett. New York: Norton, 1933.

Fromm, Erich. *The Anatomy of Human Destructiveness*. New York: Holt, Rinehart, and Winston, 1973.

Hartmann, Heinz. *Essays on Ego Psychology*. New York: International Universities Press, 1963.

————. *Psychoanalysis and Moral Values*. New York: International Universities Press, 1960.

Hiltner, Seward, and Lowell G. Colston. *The Context of Pastoral Counseling*. Nashville: Abingdon, 1961.

Hiltner, Seward, and Karl Menninger. *Constructive Aspects of Anxiety*. Nashville: Abingdon, 1963.

Hiltner, Seward. "Clinical and Theological Notes on Responsibility." *Journal of Religion and Health* 2, 1 (1962): 7–20.

————. *Pastoral Counseling*. Nashville: Abingdon. 1949.

————. *Preface to Pastoral Theology*. Nashville: Abingdon, 1983.

————. *Theological Dynamics*. Nashville: Abingdon, 1972.

Holifield, E. Brooks. *A History of Pastoral Care in America*. Nashville: Abingdon, 1983.

Horney, Karen. *Neurosis and Human Growth: The Struggle toward Self-Realization*. New York: Norton, 1950.

Hulme, William. *Pastoral Care and Counseling*. Minneapolis: Augsburg, 1981.

Hunter, Rodney. "Law and Gospel in Pastoral Care." *Journal of Pastoral Care* 30 (1976): 154.

Hyder, O. Quentin. *The Christian's Handbook of Psychiatry.* Old Tappan, N.J.: Revell, 1971.

Jones, Ernest. "Fear, Guilt, and Hate." In *Papers on Psychoanalysis.* Boston: Beacon, 1961.

Kaufman, Gershen. *Shame: The Power of Caring.* Cambridge, Mass.: Shenkman, 1980.

Kee, Howard Clark. "The Linguistic Background of 'Shame' in the New Testament." In *On Language, Culture, and Religion.* Ed. Matthew Black, 133–47. The Hague: Mouton, 1974.

Kohlberg, Lawrence. "Moral Stages and Moralization." In *Moral Development and Behavior.* Ed. T. Lickona. New York: Holt, Rinehart, and Winston, 1976.

Loomis, Earl A. *The Self in Pilgrimage.* New York: Harper, 1951.

Luther, Martin. "Answer to the Hyperchristian, Hyperspiritual, and Hyperlearned Book by Goat Emserin in Leipzig." In *Luther's Works.* Vol. 39. Philadelphia: Fortress, 1963.

———. "The Argument of St. Paul's Epistle to the Galatians." In *Luther's Works.* Vol. 26. St. Louis: Concordia, 1963.

———. "The Freedom of a Christian." In *Luther's Works.* Vol. 31, 333–77 Philadelphia: Muhlenberg, 1957.

Lynd, Helen Merrell. *On Shame and the Search for Identity.* New York: Harcourt, Brace, 1956.

May, Rollo. *Love and Will.* New York: Norton, 1969.

May, Rollo, Ernest Angel, and Henri F. Ellenberger, eds. *Existence.* New York: Basic, 1958.

McKenzie, John G. *Guilt: Its Meaning and Significance.* Nashville: Abingdon, 1962.

McNeill, John T. *A History of the Cure of Souls.* New York: Harper, 1951.

Meehl, Paul. *What, Then, Is Man?* St. Louis: Concordia, 1958.

Melanchthon, Philip. "Apology of the Augsburg Confession." *Book of Concord: Confessions of the Evangelical Lutheran Church.* Trans. Theodore G. Tappert. Philadelphia: Fortress, 1959.

Menninger, Karl. *Whatever Became of Sin?* New York: Hawthorn, 1972.

Mertz, Barbara. *Red Land, Black Land.* New York: Coward-McCann, 1966.

Morris, Leon. *The Biblical Doctrine of Judgment.* Grand Rapids: Eerdmans, 1960.

Mowrer, O. Hobart. "Alcoholics Anonymous and the 'Third' Reformation." *Religion in Life* 34 (1965): 383–97.

———. *The Crisis in Psychiatry and Religion.* Princeton: Van Nostrand, 1961.

———. *Learning Theory and Personality Dynamics.* New York: Ronald, 1950.

———. *New Group Therapy.* Princeton: Van Nostrand, 1964.

————. "The Problems of Good and Evil Empirically Considered." *Zygon* 4 (1969): 301.

————. "Science, Sex, and Values." *Personal and Guidance Journal* 42 (1964): 751.

————. "Some Constructive Features of the Concept of Sin." *Journal of Counseling Psychology* 7 (1960): 185–88.

————. "Some Philosophical Problems in Mental Disorder and Its Treatment." *Harvard Educational Review* 23 (1953): 117–27.

Narramore, Clyde Maurice. *Encyclopedia of Psychological Problems*. Grand Rapids: Zondervan, 1966.

Niebuhr, H. Richard. *The Responsible Self*. New York: Harper, 1963.

Niebuhr, Reinhold. *The Nature and Destiny of Man*. New York: Charles Scribner's Sons, 1941.

Oates, Wayne E. *The Psychology of Religion*. Waco: Word, 1973.

————. *Religious Factors in Mental Illness*. London: Allen and Unwin, 1957.

Oden, Thomas C. *Care of Souls in the Classical Tradition*. Philadelphia: Fortress, 1984.

————. *Contemporary Theology and Psychotherapy*. Philadelphia: Westminster, 1967.

————. *The Structure of Awareness*. New York: Abingdon, 1969.

————. *Pastoral Theology*. San Francisco: Harper and Row, 1983.

Odier, Charles. *Les Deux Sources, Consciento et Inconsciente, de la Via Morale*. Neuchatel: De la Baconniere, 1943.

Oglesby, William B., Jr. *Biblical Themes for Pastoral Care*. New York: Abingdon, 1980.

Oraison, Marc. *Sin: A Symposium*. New York: Macmillan, 1962.

Oxford Latin Dictionary. Vol. 1. Oxford, England: Clarendon, 1968.

Oxford English Dictionary. Vol. 2. New York: Macmillan, 1888.

Pattison, E. Mansell. *Clinical Psychiatry and Religion*. Boston: Little, Brown, 1969.

————. "On the Failure to Forgive or to Be Forgiven." *American Journal of Psychotherapy* 19 (1965): 106.

Patton, John. *Is Human Forgiveness Possible?* Nashville: Abingdon, 1985.

Peck, M. Scott. *The Road Less Traveled*. New York: Simon and Schuster, 1978.

Piaget, Jean. *The Moral Judgment of the Child*. New York: Harcourt, 1932.

Piers, Gerhard, and Milton B. Singer. *Shame and Guilt*. New York: Norton, 1971.

Pruyser, Paul. "Nathan and David: A Psychological Footnote." *Pastoral Psychology* 13 (1962): 14–18.

Quanbeck, Warren A. "Forgiveness." *The Interpreter's Dictionary of the Bible*. Ed. George A. Buttrick, et al. New York: Abingdon, 1962.

Rado, Sandor. "Emergency Behavior: With an Introduction to the Dynamics of Conscience." *Psychoanalysis and Behavior.* New York: Grune and Stratton, 1956.

Rank, Otto. *Art and Artist.* New York: Knopf, 1932.

Reik, Theodor. *The Compulsion to Confess.* New York: Farrar, Straus, and Cudahy, 1959.

Roberts, David E. *Existentialism and Religious Belief.* New York: Oxford, 1957.

Rogers, Carl R. *On Becoming a Person: A Therapist's View of Psychotherapy.* Boston: Houghton Mifflin, 1961.

Runestam, Arvid. *Psychoanalysis and Christianity.* Rock Island, Ill.: Augustana, 1932.

Salzman, Leon. "Observations on Dr. Tillich's Views of Guilt, Sin, and Reconciliation." *Journal of Pastoral Care* 11 (Spring 1957): 14–19.

Sartre, Jean Paul. *Existentialism and Human Emotions.* New York: Philosophical Library, 1958.

Schneider, Carl. *Shame, Exposure, and Privacy.* Boston: Beacon Hill, 1977.

Smedes, Lewis B. *Forgive and Forget.* New York: Harper and Row, 1984.

Stekel, Wilhelm. *Techniques of Analytical Psychotherapy.* New York: Prentice-Hall, 1959.

Switzer, David K. *Pastor, Preaching, Person.* Nashville: Abingdon, 1979.

Thurneysen, Eduard. *A Theology of Pastoral Care.* Trans. Jack A. Worthington and Thomas Wieser. Richmond: John Knox, 1962.

Tillich, Paul. *The Courage to Be.* New Haven: Yale University Press, 1952.

————. *The Dynamics of Faith.* New York: Harper, 1957.

————. "Estrangement and Reconciliation." *Review of Religion* 9 (Nov. 1944): 6–19.

————. *The Eternal Now.* New York: Scribners, 1963.

————. *Morality and Beyond.* New York: Harper and Row, 1963.

————. *Systematic Theology.* 3 vols. Chicago: University of Chicago Press, 1957.

Tournier, Paul. *The Doctor's Casebook in the Light of the Bible.* New York: Harper, 1960.

————. *Guilt and Grace.* Trans. Arthur W. Heathcote. New York: Harper, 1962.

Westermann, Claus. *Isaiah 40–66: A Commentary.* Trans. M. G. Stalker. Philadelphia: Westminster, 1969.

Williams, Daniel Day. *The Minister and the Care of Souls.* New York: Harper, 1961.

Wise, Carroll A. *Pastoral Counseling.* New York: Harper, 1951.

Index